MOTHERHOOD

The Mother of All Sexism

MOTHERHOOD
The Mother of All Sexism

A Plea for Parental Equality

Marilyse Hamelin

Translated by Arielle Aaronson

Baraka
Books

Montréal

Original edition: Maternité, *La face cachée du sexism, Plaidoyer pour l'égalité parentale* © 2017 Léméac Éditeur

© Baraka Books 2018 for the English translation (world)

ISBN 978-1-77186-137-3 pbk; 978-1-77186-165-6 epub; 978-1-77186-166-3 pdf; 978-1-77186-167-0 mobi/pocket

Book Design and Cover by Folio infographie

Editing and proofreading: Bronwyn Averett and Robin Philpot

Cover illustration: Bruce Roberts

Legal Deposit, 4th quarter 2018
Bibliothèque et Archives nationales du Québec
Library and Archives Canada

Published by Baraka Books of Montreal
6977, rue Lacroix
Montréal, Québec H4E 2V4
Telephone: 514 808-8504
info@barakabooks.com

Trade Distribution & Returns
Canada and the United States
Independent Publishers Group
1-800-888-4741 (IPG1);
orders@ipgbook.com

Printed and bound in Quebec

We acknowledge the financial support of the Société de développement des entreprises culturelles (SODEC), the Government of Quebec tax credit for book publishing administered by SODEC and the Government of Canada.

Société
de développement
des entreprises
culturelles
Québec

Funded by the Government of Canada
Financé par le gouvernement du Canada | Canadä

Contents

STILL A WOMAN'S BURDEN

Despite the substantial legal and social progress Canada has made over the past few decades with regards to gender equality, there is one area where the playing field remains woefully unequal: childcare. Women continue to bear an unequal burden which affects every single aspect of their personal and professional lives, as well as their cumulative earning power.

With her book, *Motherhood: The Mother of all Sexism*, Quebec journalist Marilyse Hamelin makes a compelling and well-researched argument about how and why motherhood continues to be a major cause of workplace discrimination, double standards, professional obstacles, guilt trips, crippling societal expectations, and immense sacrifice for women. Because of the persistent and deeply ingrained notion that women are biologically better nurturers, they are often the ones who end up relinquishing lucrative careers or personal interests to take over most child-rearing tasks.

Childcare expenses comprise the second largest expense after housing in Canada. A 2015 report by the Canadian Centre for Policy Alternatives revealed that it cost an average of $1,676 a month for infant childcare in Toronto. For many, that's a full month's salary. Why would someone work full-time only to turn around and hand over their entire pay towards childcare expenses? Since women are traditionally the ones who get compensated less, they are the ones in the family unit who often relinquish their jobs and careers to stay home and raise the kids. While a "logical" choice, it's also one imposed by gender inequity.

Hamelin understandably uses the Quebec model as a better example, since the province is ahead by leaps and bounds thanks to its universal childcare system and parental leave program. Studies have repeatedly confirmed that access to affordable childcare has had a tremendous impact on women's labour force participation rates and domestic incomes in the province.

While encouraging, this still all means very little if women continue to be stuck with the overwhelming brunt of childrearing and child-rearing-adjacent tasks (ranging from preparing lunches and dinner, taking the kids to school, homework, scheduling doctor's appointments, etc.), and housework, while having to navigate their way through a demanding work schedule and managers who question their commitment when one of the many balls they are constantly juggling occasionally drops.

While today's men are absolutely doing more than their dads did, it's still not enough. Mothers continue to be stuck with most child-related responsibilities and decisions, resulting in today's working moms being saddled with twice as many tasks and emotional labour as their stay-at-home mothers had, and often, while carrying the extra burden of being the primary caretaker for their aging parents.

"There have been so many women who stayed at home and raised the kids while men went off on adventures and pursued accomplishments," writes brilliant essayist Rebecca Solnit. "There still are. These straight men with brilliant careers and families—no one asks them how they manage to have it all, because we know: she's how."

While Quebec may indeed be more progressive than the rest of Canada in terms of paid parental leave, the five weeks of 'use it or lose it' parental benefits exclusively for fathers, and affordable childcare (not to mention affordable tuition fees that make it easier to educate children), it still pales in comparison to Nordic countries like Sweden, Denmark, and Finland.

In the meantime, young fathers who want to take on a larger role in childrearing are often prevented from doing so or discriminated against by both societal expectations and government policies that assume women are the primary caretakers.

The current system—loaded with assumptions and preassigned gender roles—isn't fair for any father who wants to truly be involved in their children's upbringing.

Hamelin said that she wrote this book so that motherhood and fatherhood would cease to be individual endeavours and private ventures. "This is a structural problem that collectively affects us all," she says, and she's right. Whether you have kids or not, how children are raised and the importance we allocate to parenting as a society affects us all in the long run. We owe it to ourselves and one another to make it as seamless and as fair as possible.

While the book will frustrate you in how it outlines what a uniquely limiting challenge motherhood can often be for women, it also inspires by offering valuable motivation on how we can collectively make things better. Both the frustration and the inspiration are necessary for change.

Toula Drimonis, June 2018

BUILDING ON QUEBEC'S EXPERIENCE IN PARENTAL EQUALITY

DEAR READERS

Quebec is a somewhat peculiar nation in North America. As early as 1997, the government set up a public network of low-cost daycares and child-care centres, known as *Centres de la petite enfance* (CPE). This had the positive impact of increasing women's employment rate. Nine years later, the government created the Quebec Parental Insurance Program by which parents can share a 32-week leave after the birth of a child. That was added to the 18-week leave for mothers and 5-week leave for fathers. Moreover, Quebec is still the only jurisdiction in North America that provides leave exclusively reserved for fathers. We could say, from this standpoint, that Quebec is an advanced society, probably the most egalitarian in North America.

Advances, however, do not mean that equality has been achieved. Quebec, like everywhere else, has to deal with the very toxic idea embedded in our collective psyche, sometimes latent, yet sometimes fully assumed, that women have some innate, instinctive, and infallible motherly knowledge about children. That belief remains the primary reason women find themselves doing most of the parenting. Women are by default the primary parent. They bear both the mental and emotional burdens, while also striving to achieve family happiness and balance.

MOM'S THERE...

This double standard in defining mothers' and fathers' roles is best illustrated by the fact that we never ask whether or not men can "have it all." And that's no wonder. When men become fathers they don't lose their specific identity. Their career success doesn't disappear in the fog. They don't wake up in the middle of stormy nights realizing that their youngest kid has probably grown out of his rubber boots, while also worrying about what to put in the lunch boxes in the morning.

Fathers get kudos for pushing their kids in strollers in the park. They are seen as the exception. Yet when they ask for a long parental leave, their employers will say *basta!* and ask them where the mother is. Our view of the father's role

is that he supports the mother. She's the fore-
woman in charge of family life.

A COSTLY IMBALANCE

The absence of shared parental responsibilities
harms women. Their independence and financial situation are compromised, as is their personal and professional fulfillment. A recent study
presented at the convention of the Association
francophone pour le savoir (ACFAS) in May 2018
revealed that childbirth results in a 40-percent
loss in income for women, but it has no financial
impact for men.

Marie Mélanie Fontaine, a co-author of the
study and doctoral student in economics at
the Université du Québec à Montréal, told the
Montreal daily *Le Devoir* that this result can
be explained by the interruptions in women's
careers, which means they accumulate less professional experience.[1] She added that women
make career choices after childbirth to obtain
greater flexibility and to take family needs into
account. But that also means less income. I would
add that some make those choices, while others
choose to leave the labour market entirely.

The same study shows that women are on
average less productive on the labour market
and less inclined to do overtime since family
responsibilities are not shared by the couple.
This is the first study to accurately measure the

financial impact of the birth of a first child and the ensuing years. These results are based on a cross-referencing of fiscal data with Statistics Canada's Longitudinal and International Study of Adults, which provides data from 1982 to 2014 on nearly 39,000 people in Canada.

Interestingly, the researchers conducted a province-by-province analysis and observed that the salary gap between women and men is less pronounced in Quebec than in the rest of Canada. Quebec's family policy has thus produced this positive result.

NOT AN ELDORADO

So Quebec does better thanks to our progressive parental support programs aimed at greater equality between parents. This certainly does not mean that gender equality has been achieved. My opinion is that we still have a long way to go.

Quebec's experience tends to show that, yes, reforms, programs, and government measures are crucial to fostering a more equitable sharing of parental responsibilities. Yet old habits and mindsets die hard, both in the general public and in the male-dominated ruling classes. Without any real political will coming from decision-makers in the upper echelons of our power structure, progress will stagnate.

Quebec's experience also reveals that strong essentialist convictions are just as pervasive as elsewhere in North America. (Essentialist here refers to the tired belief in a supposed infallible maternal instinct.) In this book, I submit that this "female know-how" is in fact the result of gender-based socialization and non-stop conditioning to which women are exposed throughout their lives.

QUEBEC AS BUILDING BLOCK

Readers in Canada and the United States will quickly realize that parental equality has not been achieved in Quebec, despite the most progressive measures in North America. At the same time, I hope that by grasping how inequalities have persisted they will draw their own conclusions and build on Quebec's experience.

My wish is that other societies inspired by the political will for greater equality will take courageous action and revolutionize parental roles by adopting measures that are even more daring than ours. Men and women are equal before the law, so time has come for women to have equal opportunity.

Marilyse Hamelin, June 2018

INTRODUCTION

DAYS OF ANGER

One cold winter morning, I sit down in front of the computer determined to work. Instead, I open Facebook and casually scroll through my newsfeed. A post by UN Women catches my eye. It's a photograph of a couple in their thirties, a man and a woman who looks to be about seven months pregnant. They are the perfect embodiment of "ambitious young professionals."

A quote from the couple, Nadia and Andrew, across the image reads, "We both want to have kids and we both want careers, too. #Planet5050." Underneath, UN Women has added "*We envisage a world where all women and girls have equal opportunities and rights by 2030.*"

It's seven o'clock in the morning, and I'm starting off my day with confirmation, as if I needed it, that women still do not have the same opportunities as men and that gender equality remains a pipe dream—a fantasy.

By 2030. How old will that make me? Exactly fifty. Part of me thinks that's much too far off; at the same time, the goal seems totally unrealistic. Dear UN Women, do you sincerely believe that in less than fifteen years everything will be settled? That we'll have achieved equality between women and men, even though this imbalance has persisted for centuries? Oh come on. If I'm sure of one thing, it's that it won't happen in my lifetime.

A silent rage creeps over me, though not directed at the UN; I've always found it stupid to shoot the messenger, especially when they're only trying to help. I put down my cup of tea and sigh. To be completely honest, I decided against having children, mostly because I wanted to see through all my projects, dreams, and ambitions. I'm not ready to risk giving all of that up just to watch from the sidelines. The last thing I want is to spend my life angry and full of regret. Angry at how society is designed for and by men, at the rampant sexism, and most of all, at my partner, whom I happen to adore. Having children likely wouldn't affect him as much. He wouldn't feel as responsible, as on-call, 24/7—old reflexes of "Mom keeps an eye out" die hard, especially if you come from a family built on the father-breadwinner/mother-home-maker model. I am certain he wouldn't have to give up his professional ambitions and dreams, or his sports and hobbies for that matter.

Once upon a time, though, I thought I wanted kids. That it was the right thing to do. Let's back up a bit. I was born in 1980. As a child, *Passe-partout*, Quebec's very popular television program, convinced me I could do anything, that I was just as good as the little boys. My parents were divorced and I would get shuttled back and forth between their homes. Joint custody went from week to week, then month to month, then year to year.

When I lived with my father, he took care of everything, from preparing meals to buying me clothes and school supplies. He even did my hair! Which is why it took me a long time to realize that an unequal division of domestic and parenting responsibilities was a widespread problem. I thought my experiences were the norm, but really they were the exception.

Much later, in my twenties and then into my thirties, when my friends, colleagues, and acquaintances started having kids, I realized that behind closed doors, things were far from equal; along with serious professional consequences, the imbalance was also standing in the way of the personal fulfilment, ambitions, and self-realization of these women. Later, as I gathered accounts printed and broadcast in the media, on blogs and across social networks, I began to realize these weren't anecdotes; it was a systemic problem. The fact is, women are discriminated against in the workplace because of their parental responsibilities.

For most women, self-sacrifice and abnegation are the natural result of motherhood. These women have internalized—probably without even knowing it—that they should be the ones making the biggest sacrifices, that this is the normal course of things, part and parcel of having children. Am I selfish to refuse to accept such unequal footing? Am I naive because I refuse to give in, to fold under pressure and just hop on the bandwagon? I am outraged in the face of injustice; I categorically refuse to play along.

Can women have it all? It's a question we never ask men, as *La Presse* columnist Nathalie Collard artfully points out. Her essay *Qui s'occupe du souper?*[1] (Who's Making Dinner?) reinforces the extent to which gender inequality persists. And a good part of gender bias originates with motherhood.

It's laughable when people claim—with a straight face, no less—that we've achieved equality, that women complain for no reason, that they are just being pains in the ass. How can one possibly be so blind, so insensitive, so self-absorbed to not only ignore the suffering of these mothers, but also to deny that it's even happening?

I am angry, wholly consumed by a desire to change the course of things. And I admit, I am steadfastly driven to pick the necessary fights. It is why I'm still a dedicated freelance journalist, despite the impracticalities of the job. If I'm seeing the glass half full, which is more or less my nature, I'd say it might be something of a productive anger. I'm a fairly pragmatic feminist and

I truly believe it is possible to change the world and the way we think, one person at a time if that's what it takes.

So Houston, we have a problem. A real one. So long as parenthood is considered an inherently feminine responsibility, we cannot achieve equal opportunity for women, all women, in the workplace or at home. Period. Not in 2030, not in 2050, not ever. I have come to this conclusion after years of research, meetings, reading, and writing, and the book you are reading is centred on this belief. Together, the different points I outline below paint a rather bleak picture.

For starters, mothers are at a disadvantage in the workforce, both in terms of employability and pay as well as career opportunities. Employers' fierce prejudices are at the root of this discrimination, in particular the widely held belief that mothers are more distracted and more inclined to miss work[2] than men. Rather than collectively investigating the underlying reasons in an attempt to remedy the situation, why not just keep blaming women, making them pay the price individually? I'm being sarcastic; it calms me down. But seriously, when a promotion is up for grabs, how do employers still consider some positions to be incompatible with motherhood, while—curiously enough—we never hear of positions that are incompatible with fatherhood?

Furthermore, women who are not mothers but who are "of childbearing age" are themselves regular victims of discriminatory hiring practices. And it's clear this window is increasing thanks to assisted reproductive technology. Discrimination occurs when employers assume these women want to start a family sooner or later and opt straightaway for a male applicant who won't "let down the company" by taking off on "maternity leave."[3] Not to mention the fact that, during a job interview,[4] many potential employers ask applicants if they plan to have children, although this is officially prohibited by Quebec's *Charter of Human Rights and Freedoms*. We all know that women have an annoying habit of getting pregnant the moment they get hired, right? Ugh, seriously? This antiquated notion that having children is the selfish lot of unfortunate women rather than a life goal with a positive impact for society as a whole . . . it really makes my blood boil.

How many mothers have their applications brushed aside before even being granted an interview because of that "hole" in their CV for those few years they stayed home to take care of their children? A recent profile in the magazine *Les affaires* made me wince when it lauded the professional achievements of an entrepreneur whose business travels took him all over the globe. He was lucky enough to have the support of his partner, who had put her own career on hold to take care of their children.[5] Their situation was presented as an ideal partnership, an inspiration. Are you kidding? It must be easy to strike a healthy work-family balance when the woman is encouraged to give up her own career ambitions.

Granted, this is one couple's personal decision; it's important to note that a minority of fathers also choose to put their careers on hold to take care of the children. But how can you ignore the fact that it is still women who, in the vast majority of cases, take parental leave, willingly reduce their work hours and, in some cases, opt out of the labour market, to devote themselves to their kids? What happens when they decide to opt back in—to gain financial independence and avoid having to rely on a partner to guarantee a decent retirement? Will they, too, suffer from the hole-in-the-CV syndrome?

Despite legislative gains making it illegal for employers to fire pregnant women (though it still happens![6]) and requiring them to reintegrate employees post-parental leave, women who stop working to take care of children still pay the price, because *de jure* equality doesn't translate into de facto equality. Even with a standard parental leave, these women risk having their biggest accounts handed over to colleagues in their absence. If they take extended leave and decide not to go back to work, they will have to justify this temporary pause, this "blemish," to future employers, as if helping educate the next generation of citizens constituted a crime of non-productivity. We've all seen it—when it comes to hiring practices, even women with no children pay the professional price of motherhood-related sexism, whether or not they want a family.

This is why motherhood (lived or not), and the fact of being a woman, represents serious social and professional inequities for all women—consequences that will be felt throughout life. Jobs, promotions, pay raises, and any other missed opportunities account for dead losses that echo throughout careers and into retirement. In short, motherhood-related discrimination in the workplace systemically impacts all women, whether or not they are mothers and regardless of their age.

In October 2015, Stéphanie Grammond, finance columnist at *La Presse*, reported that women represent the poorer parent in retirement. "Their revenue accounts for just 59 percent of men, or $27,200 compared to $45,800. This disparity reflects the fact that women earn chronically lower salaries throughout their career. . . . Earnings for women in Quebec only represent 71 percent of their male counterparts. Despite an established pay equity, their hourly salary remains 10 percent below male earners. And women are underrepresented in the workforce too, as they are more likely to be caregivers for children or sick relatives."[7] Grammond does point out that the Québec Pension Plan (QPP) allows women to partially compensate for their non-remunerated work by deducting the years during which they made few contributions due to caring for a child. In spite of these measures, QPP payments are much lower for women, due in part to the persistent wage gap, but also to missed opportunities for career advancement, since our so-called modern society still considers women the heads of the home and family sphere.

And don't tell me that women are OK with this, that deep down they don't want promotions, preferring instead to take care of the family. In September 2016, L'effet A initiative,[8] in collaboration with *Châtelaine* magazine, published the results of a survey showing that women in Quebec have as much professional ambition as men (73 percent of women reported being ambitious, versus 78 percent of men[9]).

When asked what held them back, women naturally cited family obligations, but not as the main obstacle (family was fourth place). To them, the central problem was how they felt overlooked and often excluded when it came time to hand out promotions. Ironically, male respondents tended to think family obligations were the number-one hurdle when it came to women's professional ambition. But what both male and female survey respondents expressed is essentially two sides of the same coin. If women are overlooked—in other words, if they lack opportunities for climbing the career ladder compared to their male colleagues—, it's because these mostly male decision-makers still adhere, consciously or not, to the notion that for women, family comes first.

And it's not just employers who consider women to be the default parent. It is often still the case with male partners, whether they are conscious of this or not. And as long as mothers are considered the go-to parent, there will never be true equality in terms of children's care and education, or household duties. And this unbalanced division of responsibilities in the private sphere creates a heavy mental load for working mothers; these women must perform at the level of their male colleagues and even beyond, since women still bear the burden of proof[10] when it comes to workplace competence.

Systemic discrimination, wage loss, and job insecurity—this is the sobering picture of motherhood. I hope these pages will spark debate and shine a light on this still-unresolved issue of our time, bringing it into the public arena. More than anything, I want to help women—all women. There are lots of concrete ways to solve the problem, which I will detail in the following chapters.

CHAPTER I

MOTHERHOOD AND THE JOB MARKET: THE DOMINION OF DISCRIMINATION

Everyone knows that good mothers, true "Mother Courages," know no sacrifice too small for their brood. This is the dominant model, the one our society promotes: shame on any mother who refuses to conform. With this in mind, I could list all types of career "choices" which aren't really choices, the ones mothers make to cope with family life, such as putting in fewer hours, working closer to home, turning down a promotion, and more. And this doesn't take into account all the sacrifices that aren't choices.

Take the story of one mother of two young children, who periodically needed to take off work due to family obligations. While this woman, who wishes to remain anonymous, has worked for a large media company for over a decade, she still does not have job security. Yet over the years she has stopped counting the number of men just starting their careers who, without family or other attachments preventing them from working countless hours, have quickly surpassed her and secured permanent positions. If you look past the lip service and righteous sermons we keep hearing about work-life balance, what does this reveal about our society? Work trumps all, so much for reconciling career with family; that's a private affair, a mother's personal problem. Let them deal with the issue!

Another mother who also works at a media company had her position eliminated at the end of her maternity leave. And since she had not earned revenue over the previous fifty-two weeks, she was not eligible for unemployment benefits. To put it bluntly, she got screwed. She was lucky enough to have a partner who was able to support her financially while she looked for a job. But what about when this happens to a single mother? How is it possible that mothers in this situation have no recourse? Shouldn't such circumstances warrant admissibility for employment insurance? Even people in prison awaiting trial have better luck: they are eligible for unemployment benefits if found not guilty. Our social safety net is there to attenuate unfortunate situations. Wouldn't losing your job during parental leave apply? It seems as though, once again, mothers are left behind.

Sometimes employers use another dirty, sexist trick by assuring the mother-to-be not to worry, that her job will be waiting for her when she gets back—only to eliminate it in a sideways manner. This is what happened to a friend's sister, who thought she had settled things before leaving. Since her office was in Montreal and she lived across the bridge on the South Shore, her employer had agreed to let her work from home for half the time, a positive solution often used to promote healthy work-family balance. But one week before her return to work, he simply changed his mind. The new mother, unsure how she could manage a new baby and a full-time job in Montreal, resigned. And you guessed it: no unemployment benefits for her either. Screwed once again.

I don't know whether her partner tried to negotiate work-family arrangements with his own employer (such as working remotely) or whether, faced with a hypothetical refusal, he would have also thought about resigning, but I doubt it. Why is it the mother's responsibility to make this type of sacrifice right from the get-go? How can we make it so the father feels equally responsible?

Another mother who worked for a multi-national telecommunications firm returned from maternity leave only to find her largest accounts had been permanently reassigned to her colleagues, the "reliable" employees, i.e. those without children. For more than a year she was shelved, given insignificant jobs while she sweat it out, punished for betraying the company by daring to take advantage of parental leave.

And what of the candour, to put it nicely, of the former editor-in-chief of a well-known daily who, several years ago, told a journalist fresh off her second parental leave that he no longer trusted her? Incidentally, she has since applied again and again to become an editor, to no avail; she's a model employee now stuck in her current position with no chance of advancement.

Speaking of the promotions women are denied once they have children, here's another jaw-dropper. The scene: a popular Quebec magazine, an employee a few months pregnant. The team lead position becomes available. Not only does the woman have all the requisite skills and degrees, but she also has years of experience at the company. So she decides to apply. Meanwhile, the employer posts her position externally in preparation for her temporary maternity leave. And that's when a young man straight out of university with no professional experience applies for the maternity leave replacement. Which position do you think he landed? You got it—team lead! He became the immediate supervisor of the experienced employee who, to add insult to injury, was not even asked to an interview for the position.

Some people may be familiar with a September 2016 article in *Le Devoir*[1] chronicling how Évelyne

Bourdua-Roy, a young female doctor, was paid 15 percent less than her male colleagues for having failed to meet the patient quota required in the first year of practice. Because she got pregnant and went out on maternity leave mid-year. You read that right. The law does not consider pregnancy a valid reason for failing to hit the 500-patient requirement during the first year of practice.

You might argue that Bourdua-Roy could have timed her pregnancy better. First, who says it was planned? I know women who've gotten pregnant while they had an IUD and their partner was wearing a condom. In the fertility lottery (and that of bad luck), not everyone has the same odds. But even if it was a planned pregnancy, why should she be penalized when the law could have made an exception for pregnant women? What kind of message does that send? You could contend that we're talking about first-world problems, that doctors earn a good living, that missing out on a bonus is not the end of the world. But my point is that gender equality must apply to every situation. No woman should experience a dip in income because she had a baby, period. Quebec's *Charter of Human Rights and Freedoms* prohibits discrimination based on pregnancy and declares that no woman is to be treated differently because she is pregnant or on maternity leave.

Another thing I found disheartening about this particular case was the reaction of Quebec's union of general practitioners, the FMOQ. Communications director Jean-Pierre Dion explicitly told a *Devoir* journalist that the organization had not anticipated Bourdua-Roy's situation when it adopted the new Quebec measures. And women are left behind once again!

I'd like to point out that such bonuses don't take into account the fact that women doctors choose to work fewer hours in the interest of balancing work and family life, and therefore see fewer patients. The result, you can guess, is that it is overwhelmingly the male doctors who are benefiting from this incentive. Once again, decisions are being made by and for men that fail to consider women's circumstances.

I could go on and on, and I'm sure you've got some pretty unbelievable anecdotes as well. Most women can rattle off a slew of infuriating stories featuring maternity-related discrimination, and they're quick to tell me their own, or that of a friend. Overlooked, punished, pushed to one side, the stories abound. I've collected dozens since beginning research for this book. The problem is beyond anecdotal; it is systemic.

After publishing the book *Women and Power: The Case For Parity,*[2] journalist Pascale Navarro has continued to vocalize that men, too, should feel concerned by problems of equality and that so-called "female" issues needed to become issues for all. Unfortunately, we aren't there yet. I'd go so far as to say it's a long road ahead, both for decision-makers and in popular culture and attitudes.

Journalist Louise Gendron published a long interview between Louis Morissette and Éric Salvail in *Châtelaine*'s June 2015 issue in which the pair of artist/entrepreneurs spoke about managing human resources in addition to being TV producers. When the subject of maternity leave came up, there was an unmistakable flash of latent sexism.

> Louis Morissette: The other thing I find tough is human resources. Office disagreements, the girl who gets pregnant—you're happy for her, but at the same time . . .
> Éric Salvail: They've just put you in deep sh--!

The fact that it's spelled out in a magazine intended for a female audience, without any further explanation or context offered,[3] without a nod to the sexist and discriminatory content—written by a woman, I think it important to note—says a lot about just how far we are from a shift in attitudes.[4]

I understand the challenge parental leave poses for small- and medium-sized businesses, but can we come up with solutions instead of treating each case like an isolated problem? You'd think having children were an accident, an anomaly, where it should be the norm—news to be welcomed and embraced.

What if recruitment agencies specialized in this niche? After all, businesses don't shoulder the financial burden of replacing an employee out on parental leave, since benefits are covered by the Quebec Parental Insurance Plan (QPIP). The person filling in must be available on short notice, requiring some form of job training, but given that a baby's due date is known months in advance (except in cases of preventive leave in early pregnancy, a situation that does not affect fathers-to-be), finding a replacement should not be that complicated for the employer. More importantly, it shouldn't be perceived so negatively, as the proverbial thorn in one's side.

How can we make it so that a baby announcement is welcome news or, at the very least, considered a part of life instead of a problem to be solved? This kind of attitude stigmatizes women and makes securing employment more difficult. And it's not unrelated to the fact that the Liberal government in Québec, receptive to the grievances of the Conseil du patronat du Québec (Quebec's leading business lobby) and other like-minded business networks, feels justified in considering reducing funding for non-discriminatory programs like the QPIP.

A DISTINCT SOCIETY?

Since 2006, the Quebec Parental Insurance Plan has been providing new parents across Quebec with benefits that greatly exceed those of parents in other Canadian provinces.[5] These other provinces still rely on employment insurance, while Quebec chose to repatriate this money.

But the Quebec program is not perfect. It excludes parents who have been deemed insufficient contributors before the birth of their child, which rules out benefits for students living off loans and bursaries. And what do you think happens to these parents when they have to put their studies on hold to take care of an infant? You guessed it, screwed again! They aren't eligible for either parental benefits or for loans or bursaries.

Nevertheless, when the Quebec program was established it was a small revolution in terms of managing parental leave, and no one has ever looked back. But this doesn't mean we should sit back and admire the status quo. I don't believe the government should take a step back, reduce benefits, or even adopt a non-interventionist approach when it comes to parenthood. Quite the contrary—it must invest further. I'll revisit this idea in Chapter 4 and in the conclusion.

Quebec has established flagship programs when it comes to balancing work and family life: I am referring to the QPIP—the only program of its kind in North America—and its network of public daycares, Centres de petite enfance (CPEs). They are the product of a joint fight led by feminist groups and trade unions. But what some see as gains are nonetheless undermined, if not outright challenged by employers working to limit their implementation. Just think of preventive leave for pregnant employees, one achievement that is constantly being questioned. And when we compare the QPIP to other programs across the world, we are lagging behind the Scandinavian nations and other countries in Europe. However, like the single uniform price in child-care centres (CPEs), the program nearly bore the brunt of Quebec Premier Phillippe Couillard's austerity measures.

In September 2015, the government announced a 2 percent drop in QPIP contributions beginning January 2016, opening the door to possible cuts to a program having experienced past deficits.[6] In an article published in the *Journal de Montréal* announcing the decrease in funding, comments by the Canadian Federation of Independent Business (CFIB) clearly indicated they were delighted. According to François Vincent, CFIB's Director of Provincial Affairs:

> To promote Quebec's economic development, we must give our SMEs room to grow so they can invest according to their needs, their reality, and their priorities. We hope the government will continue to ease the economic burden of SMEs, as it is doing currently, to encourage economic growth and job creation.

It's clear that equal employment opportunities for women don't carry much weight when it comes to economic development.

The following month, journalist Noémie Mercier reported in the magazine *L'actualité* that

Ankita Patnaik, economist at Cornell University, concluded that the QPIP, and paternity leave in particular, had contributed to rebalancing roles for fathers and mothers in Quebec, both inside and outside of the home, encouraging mothers to remain in the workforce.[7] Mercier writes that, "fathers of young children surveyed in 2010 spent an increase of twenty-two minutes per day taking care of the children and an extra fifteen minutes doing housework," adding that "these thirty-seven minutes represent a 23 percent increase over pre-reform era fathers."

Of course a *rebalancing* is neither panacea nor equality, but rather a decrease in the inequalities when it comes to sharing household responsibilities that, as we have already seen, remain a reality. Nevertheless, the introduction of the QPIP in 2006 was a first step—a leap, really—in the right direction and I see no advantages to making cuts to a program contributing to the edification of a more just, equitable, and egalitarian society.

And Ms. Patnaik isn't the only one south of the border interested in our parental leave program. The Center for American Progress heralded it as "one of the best in the world" because it is aimed at both women and men.[8] Sarah Jane Glynn, Director of Women's Economic Policy at the Center, explained in an interview with the Quebec City daily *Le Soleil*, "when policies are directed solely or especially at women, we see that even if it's illegal, companies tend to hire fewer women to avoid having to pay for maternity leave." She adds that, "in contrast to the strictly pro-birth agenda of other countries with maternity leave benefits, Quebec's policy of shared leave between parents also aims to promote gender equality." It's no accident the birth rate in Quebec has experienced a slight increase since the program's inception.

Let me be clear: I hate when politicians guilt and pressure women into having more children. And I'm no fan of diehard economic arguments and columns of numbers that have an annoying tendency to ignore human variables in the real world, where things can't always be quantified. That said, a program such as the QPIP that helps women better reconcile career with children is valuable from a birthrate, and therefore economic, standpoint. In fact, Valérie Harvey, Ph.D. candidate in sociology at the Université Laval, summed up her thesis in an open letter published by *La Presse* in September 2014:

> We now know that the combination of subsidized daycares and parental leaves has significantly impacted the Quebec birth rate. Eight years after the QPIP was established, the statistics still prove encouraging (1.65 children in 2013). According to the Institut de la statistique du Québec, fertility rates after 2006 are the highest they have been since 1980! . . . Do we want to reduce a birth rate that is still under the replacement fertility rate (2.1 children per woman)?[9]

Quebec's program leads to a better, albeit still flawed, division of labour and parental responsibilities, helps women balance career and family life, improves the birth rate—making it a good long-term investment—and the government wants to slash the budget? How can we be so blind? Would cuts to the QPIP even be on the table if the predominantly male decision-makers felt as though issues of parenthood, and by extension, equality, would impact them? Or is it that they know the cuts won't make waves since the domestic and familial spheres continue to be treated as a secondary concern, a woman's responsibility? I think the answer is obvious.

BALANCING WORK AND FAMILY: THE EMPLOYER PERSPECTIVE

Letting companies take care of their employees when it comes to balancing work and family life is risky business. For Rachel Chagnon, law professor at the Université du Québec à Montréal (UQAM) and the director of its research and women's studies institute, the IREF, it's naively optimistic to think companies will simply do the right thing:

> There is an entrepreneurial narrative that says "we can self-regulate, self-organize." Companies only do this when they are required to, otherwise they'll do whatever is most lucrative for them, with no particular regard for their employees. There are plenty of industrial psychologists working tirelessly to

convince employees they are happy, even if those employees aren't treated particularly well.[10]

There are a handful of scheduling adjustments that employers can implement, such as flexible hours or the ability to work remotely. But in rare cases where these options do exist, it is still mostly women who take advantage of them, even today. This is what Chagnon calls the "internalization of inequalities by women themselves." And the same goes for the longer parental leave, transferrable in theory but still utilized by mothers in the vast majority of cases.

Chagnon nevertheless believes that the QPIP has been an excellent development in terms of providing job security for women with stable employment, allowing these women to maintain contact with their work environment and preventing them from becoming financially dependent:

> We want women to have children, it's good for society, but at the same time we need to understand that it's a sacrifice that should be recognized. This is no insignificant thing; the QPIP was a landmark step that has helped countless women.[11]

I would be remiss if I didn't mention that the Quebec program has had detrimental side effects; it has created new forms of discrimination among working mothers, some of whom are cast aside upon their return to the office. In reality this is the same old sexism that, much like a virus, changes form and persists under new conditions.

Chagnon believes the parental leave system could be improved by ensuring accessibility for even the most vulnerable employees, particularly women working in the service industry. "Even if these workers have access in theory, they won't take parental leave because they are dealing with delinquent employers who will punish them in some way if they do," she notes.

Chagnon divides employees into two types: those who have stable, full-time employment that gives them access to the QPIP, and those sometimes qualified as the lumpenproletariat,[12] a sector that is steadily growing and includes employees of retail giants—who employ a lot of women—, employment agencies, or the social economy sector, such as home aid workers, where women's schedules are irregular and often given only a week in advance, if that.

> These employees do not know ahead of time when they will get time off and if they will be able to take it when needed. For example, if they decide to take a day off because their child has a dentist appointment, they risk losing their job and have virtually no recourse. And if after getting their schedule these women refuse to work on a given day, their hours will be halved and they'll find themselves at the bottom of the list. In these types of jobs, access to a full-time schedule is based on seniority. The employer prefers part-time hours since it

allows for a more flexible schedule, but this affords employees little to no job security.[13]

Chagnon notes that poor working conditions make it impossible to maintain a healthy family life. She points out that on average, these women take one or two months' leave after the birth of a child:

> They rarely take more than three months, out of financial need. They may not lose their job, but they will lose priority and risk having their hours reduced to almost nothing. So we can fine-tune existing measures like the QPIP and give more time to the father—this is great, it's absolutely an improvement—, but there's a whole group of women workers being neglected, whose working conditions are overlooked.[14]

Chagnon offers a much-needed wake-up call. We forget about these vulnerable workers when we keep demanding more for the middle class, but they exist too. And they would also like access to parental leave. But where would they find the time to fight for their rights, to catch the eye of decision-makers, when they are struggling to survive financially? Remember that being a feminist means wanting equality for *all* women. But mothers without job security working at minimum wage get left behind.

The *Act Respecting Labour Standards* states that "at the end of a maternity, paternity or parental leave, the employer shall reinstate the employee in the employee's former position with the same benefits, including the wages to which the employee would have been entitled had the employee remained at work." But nowhere does it specifically mention hours or seniority or recall lists, which opens the door to bad faith interpretations.

We must crack down on delinquent employers who demand workers' absolute availability and threaten to drop them down the priority list when they need to miss work due to family obligations or while out on parental leave.[15] These cautionary punishments aim to dissuade women workers from claiming their rights. These are blatant cases of discrimination related to parenthood and, let's face it, in most cases motherhood.

Quebec's work, health, safety and equity board, La Commission des normes, de l'équité, de la santé et de la sécurité du travail (CNESST), currently serves the passive role of handling individual complaints; instead of settling for this, could we not give this government body the means to adopt a proactive approach to offending employers, whose abuses are often systematic?

This could include sending agents into the workplace on random inspections of retail companies to interview employees and gather information. Fining offending employers could help finance this project within the CNESST.

If you have ever filed a complaint with the standards board, the CNESST, you know that

it is a long and potentially discouraging process. Moreover, once the grievance is filed,
the Commission contacts the employer for an
interview. This may prompt aggrieved workers
labouring in non-unionized environments where
managing staff is often an arbitrary affair to fear
reprisal by the employer. There should be an
option to file an anonymous complaint with the
CNESST that would include an on-site visit as part
of the investigation.

I am also concerned about where the so-called
sharing economy will lead, when anyone can be
their own boss and work around the clock just
to make ends meet. These admirable initiatives
across web and mobile platforms allow people to
deliver pizza, offer massage therapy services, or
provide taxi rides, with zero job protection, paid
vacation, or sick days—all the hard-earned advances of wage earners throughout the 20th century. Is that really where our economy is heading?
Workers caught in the each-to-his-own mentality,
at the hands of supply and demand? I fear the
worst when it comes to the work-life balance of
future generations of parents. As Rachel Chagnon
so aptly put it, "we'll all win the right to exploit
ourselves."

CHAPTER 2

WHY ARE MOTHERS STILL THE DEFAULT PARENT?

It's a warm day near the end of May, and I'm having a drink outside with a girlfriend in her early 30s. She tells me about how a few years ago, while living with a man who had custody of his son, the child assistance payment the government sent in the mail was issued in her name. She wasn't the child's mother, so why on earth was it in her name and not the father's? I was shocked; it seemed unbelievable.

After some research, it appears that it's standard practice for Ottawa to send the child assistance payments[1] to the woman in the couple, regardless of whether or not she is the mother. In fact, the *Income Tax Act* is doubly sexist by virtue of the "female presumption rule."[2] For families where the parents are still together, it assumes that the female parent is the parent responsible for the care and education of the children. As a result, the cheque is automatically issued to the mother. But the law also considers the father's spouse or common-law partner as the parent of his children "in the broader sense," which explains why the government issues the cheque in her name.

It goes without saying that this "female presumption rule" helps perpetuate the notion that caring for children is a woman's domain. It's no wonder, given these conditions, mothers are riddled with guilt and feel responsible for everything within the domestic and family sphere—even the government reinforces the idea!

A few weeks after our drink, my friend admitted that even though she wasn't the child's mother, she actually did do more on a daily basis when it came to cooking meals, doing laundry, buying school supplies, and so on. "I'm definitely not the first step-mom to do this," she allowed. "In the end, you wonder if the government isn't right in assuming who does the shopping and who actually takes care of the children." I answer that it's the age-old question of the chicken or the egg. Women do perform a greater share of the childcare, but this is a social construct we need to dismantle. The government should work on eliminating this stereotype instead of reinforcing it.

As I've written before, including on my blog[3] and for the magazine *Planète F*,[4] mothers are constantly preoccupied with thoughts of family. Moms are generally the ones who keep the kids' health insurance cards in their wallets, who manage the family schedule, and plan meals and activities, all in addition to working outside of the home, often full-time.

A 2015 report entitled "Pour un partage équitable du congé parental" (toward an equitable division of parental leave) published by the Quebec's Council on the Status of women, the Conseil du statut de la femme (CSF), notes that despite women flooding the labour market over the past fifty years, they still perform an average of 70 percent of the housework and childcare.[5]

According to 35-year-old Marianne Prairie, author, blogger, family and parenting speaker, and mother of two young children, our society as a whole entrusts women to be the keepers of the domestic and parental spheres. As proof, the workshops she co-organizes with Odile Archambault on helicopter parenting, work-family balance, and the importance of creating parent networks draw what she describes as a "99.9 percent female" audience, even when held outside working hours.

Obviously in single-parent families[6] headed by women,[7] the mother alone is in charge of organizing the family. But for the majority of heterosexual couples, the mother is still the first responder or "default parent" if you will. "The system is set up so that mom is the indispensable parent, creating a sense of guilt for working mothers," Prairie argues. The general anxiety mothers feel doesn't come out of nowhere—women are cogs in a well-oiled machine, their minds constantly on overdrive to keep up.

The most recent data indicates that women in Quebec take off work nearly twice as often as men for family obligations.[8] Yet among those with children under sixteen, 82 percent are employed.[9] Why do these responsibilities fall to them? Prairie notes:

> Often it's a habit developed over the course of maternity leave. The majority of women take the long parental leave and many breastfeed. This head start when it comes to family organization and childcare extends after women return to work. The mother becomes the primary parent by default.[10]

Prairie adds that popular culture spreads the belief that mothers are better equipped to take care of children since parenting books are primarily geared toward women:

> There is a critical mass of information targeting women specifically, whether it is invitations to join a mommy Facebook group, advertisements in general, hospital mailing lists following childbirth, etc. In the end, it's the mother who knows how much diapers cost or the best brand of baby formula.[11]

I also believe that the long parental leave, taken by women in the vast majority of cases (and often wrongly referred to as maternity leave), perpetuates the myth of Mother Courage and locks women into the role of primary parent.

I was pleased to come across an account by Marie Pagès, a Quebec social worker who was on parental leave when she wrote an open letter[12] published in *Le Devoir*. In it, Pagès denounces the insidious avenues through which women on maternity leave wind up in social spaces such as cooking, stroller fitness, zumba, or mommy-baby yoga classes, sewing workshops, and discussion groups on motherhood, along with breastfeeding clinics offered by local community service centres (CLSCs) that aim to transform women into perfect mothers in body and mind:

> Claiming to produce programming that meets the wants and needs of mothers, these spaces do much more than break the isolation of women at home; they shape the mothers of today. Women become not mothers, but experts in motherhood. Thanks to CPR courses, breastfeeding support clinics, and sleep workshops, they wind up being responsible not only for the primary needs of the baby—health, nutrition, and sleep—but also for making sure baby cultivates good motor and social skills and demonstrates healthy psychosexual development. And to make sure peace reigns everywhere, mom also has free access to various workshops on maintaining a healthy sex life, building relationships with grandparents, and facilitating sibling harmony. These experts on motherhood—the nutritionists, seamstresses, nurses, housekeepers, occupational therapists, and full-time distributors of unconditional love—are ready to answer all your questions. Blogs, Facebook groups, and more won't fail to point out

that you must know how to meet your baby's needs at all times. With every notification you'll be bombarded with photos ("think it's eczema?"), advertisements ("I just bought X stroller, I couldn't live without it!"), questions ("he's six months old, can I give him grapes?"), worries ("she's nine months old and isn't walking yet, is this normal?"), and big victories ("we finally got the baby to sleep six hours straight!"). It's worse than it was for mothers of past generations because today, mothers think they have the freedom to make choices.[13]

We also have to look at how mainstream media that specializes in content for parents such as *Enfants Québec, Yoopa,* or *Maman pour la vie* talk to mothers. By addressing mothers almost exclusively, these local magazines and webzines only further the problem. Of course, it's a vicious circle. If fathers aren't interested in reading or contributing to these publications because they don't feel concerned by issues of parenthood, we haven't made any headway. Once again, we're in a catch-22.

The independent Quebec web-based media company *Planète F* tackles the parenthood question from an egalitarian standpoint by bringing together journalists and bloggers of both genders. Meanwhile, other increasingly popular sites like *Maman a un plan,* co-authored by Marianne Prairie, or *TPL Moms* by twins Josiane and Carolane Stratis, almost exclusively[14] give a platform to female voices. And yet these are feminist publications offering very progressive points of view. I am certainly not pointing any fingers—just the opposite!—since these sites are helpful and pertinent, but the question remains: can't we make more room for male voices so we can also talk about paternity?

Marianne Prairie explains that her blog *Maman a un plan* (Mom has a plan) presents a candid, egalitarian, and active vision of parenting "to put things out there, so they change." It nevertheless has a 95 percent female readership and I wonder if the rather gendered name plays a role. Can fathers feel comfortable reading a blog called *Maman a un plan*? Why not go with something more neutral?

I put on my white gloves to ask Prairie— whom I admire and who is, after all, cofounder of the site *Je suis féministe* (I am a feminist)—the thorny question: Isn't there a certain irony to the title, considering how often women lament that parenthood is perceived as a uniquely feminine responsibility? "As women, we can only share our reality as mothers," she tells me. "There is already so much to study, shake up, and dust off when it comes to motherhood. We address issues of motherhood as well as relationship equality."

I ask about possibly including dad bloggers in order to bring the conversation about masculinity and paternity to a new place. "We'd love to hear from the dads, let them take the floor. It'd be good for everyone," she adds. "But do I have to carve out a spot for them on my own blog?"

She's got a point. Nothing is stopping Quebec fathers from launching a blog on fatherhood. But is it realistic, given the social construct surrounding parenthood that immediately establishes the mother as primary, default parent? All the more reason, I would argue, to give men space to change this perception.

I dug around and came across a handful of blogs (of varying quality) where fathers wrote about parenthood. In the category "sensitive and touching personal account" there is children's author François Bérubé, while bloggers Blaise Durivage, Jean-François Quessy, and Jean-Félix Maynard take a lighter, more humorous tone. And then I read a magnificent piece by Marc-André Durocher, blogger for *Planète F*.[15] Here's an excerpt:

> We live in a patriarchal society, and it's problematic. Every time I interact with a woman, I'm consciously trying to change the existing power dynamic. Especially on a daily basis with my partner. This makes me unusual. I know it, I see it, and I recognize it. Our sexist system favours the fathers, and we're comfortable with that. Given this, it's easy to understand why the men I know act the way they do. They haven't even begun to think about these issues. It's easier to let their partner take a day off when Benjamin is sick. Get involved when it comes to sports and other fun activities. Give children their last name, because that's the norm. Let their partner cook dinner, even though she's tired after a long day at work. Because "it tastes

better when she cooks." It's easier to deal with the people around you when you fit the image of the "dad next door." It's less confrontational, you don't have to keep questioning yourself.

A MOTHER'S INVISIBLE WORK

In most unions, the mother bears the mental burden of household planning. So I ask Olivier Lamalice, a researcher with Quebec's Council on the Status of Women and author of the report on an equitable division of parental leave, to talk to me about this invisible work. He tells me that, interestingly enough, it's impossible to collect data on the mental strain linked to household planning, even though everyone acknowledges its existence. He explains:

> If we look solely at the statistics on the division of labour within couples, there's clearly been an improvement. Between 1986 and 2010, men have increased the amount of time spent caring for children and women have slightly reduced time spent on household chores. But there's still a gap. And free time has dropped dramatically for women, especially for those with children under four. For them it equates to an hour and a half less free time a day since 1986, mainly because they spend more time working outside the home and their household duties have not decreased proportionately.[16]

An hour and a half a day is huge! By the end of the week, these mothers are losing ten and a half hours of free time. Say goodbye to your hobbies! Lamalice continues:

> We can't quantify the mental load, in the same way we can't measure multitasking. The person responsible for meal planning, staying in contact with daycare or school, going to the doctor—generally the mother—often works as well. She might spend her lunch hour making phone calls. By comparison, the partner who is assigned responsibilities does not devote much mental space to these chores. You don't spend a day planning out how to mow the lawn. And if we look at traditionally male-dominated jobs such as home renovation, the planning involved is so temporary that at a certain point it stops adding up. When a project is done, it's done.[17]

At this point in the conversation I remember a former colleague who would take her lunch break to go shopping for dinner—which she also cooked, of course—while her boyfriend spent his going to the gym. They were a young couple in their thirties, the kind we are counting on to change things. And I'm certain that either has yet to recognize the blatant inequality of their partnership.

Is it possible to get fathers to share an equal part of the burden of planning responsibilities? It is, but Marianne Prairie would argue it is extremely difficult; she believes that division of labour depends on how you were raised: "The couples I know with the greatest equality have men who grew up in feminist households. It isn't as apparent in the beginning of a relationship, but their behaviour really takes shape once kids are in the picture."

Rachel Chagnon argues that since logistical organization secures a family's well-being, in some ways mothers shoulder the burden of keeping their family happy. She adds that it is a "fundamental issue—no relationship can be equal as long as only one person is doing the planning." I agree with her, and I would add that women will never achieve equality, not in their private lives, and not in the workforce. That is the whole premise of this book.

Employers aren't blind to the burden of family organization that falls to mothers; as I wrote in the introduction, it is the reason women are less attractive to hire and to promote. But penalizing female workers would be to go back the way we came by perpetuating the discrimination that has existed since women first joined the workforce. It should be just the opposite; in addition to recognizing working mothers and establishing ways to reconcile work-family balance, we must insist that these measures address more than just the woman. Fathers should be encouraged to take longer parental leave, just as they should be calling out of work because the baby got an ear infection at daycare. The mental weight of familial responsibilities and organization must be shared equally, once and for all.

MOMS DO IT ALL

In the previous chapter, I discussed the repro-
duction of everyday sexism. The old double standards that make us, consciously or not, think of
a mother's caregiving as normal, expected, and
taken for granted while the same caregiving is
considered spectacular when it comes from the
father.

Rachel Chagnon condemns this phenomenon, which she sees as one-sided positive
reinforcement:

> As a mother, you praise your children when they
> make their beds and do their share of the chores,
> just like you praise your partner for cooking every
> other week or taking the kids to play in the park,
> but everything you do is normal, it's expected. At
> the end of the day, it's always the same people get-
> ting rewarded and feeling appreciated.[18]

When I argue, as many do, that parental leave
should be shared more equally between parents,
it certainly isn't to congratulate dad for being a
superhero. And yet! According to Chagnon, men
receive more help when raising a young child
or baby, both from their spouse and mother as
well as from their friends, which lets them do
things other than childcare. To illustrate her
point, Chagnon references a study conducted by
Francine Descarries:

Francine Descarries, professor emeritus at UQAM's sociology department and former director of IREF, conducted a 2007-2008 study on student parents, both couples and single parents. What stood out was that with couples—and again, we're talking about 2007-2008, not 1958—the division of labour was more egalitarian in quantitative terms but hardly at all in qualitative terms. The more fun or rewarding tasks, like bath time, daycare pick-up, playing, and going to the park, were the man's responsibility. Because, you know, it's so great that they're getting involved! But the most unpleasant tasks, like washing diapers, and logistical details, such as packing lunches, remained the woman's responsibility. Apart from taking care of the lawn, the shovelling, and the trash, men wound up with more rewarding chores.[19]

I think of Olivier Lamalice's 2015 field study for the status of women report, which I will return to in Chapters 3 and 4: the conclusions are identical. Things haven't changed a bit.

There's no quick fix, argues Chagnon, for this damn double standard. Francine Descarries notes that her research included studying single fathers and mothers:

Single fathers systematically received more help, particularly from their own mother. Mothers are more likely to help a son than a daughter. Because women are considered competent in their role as mothers.

I see this as an essentialist position many still defend today: that women have an innate ability to parent. Chagnon agrees with me, though she adds that many women play into this notion by making themselves indispensable. "I've seen extreme cases, women with nearly full-grown children who can't leave for a weekend without filling the fridge, convinced that things would fall apart if they didn't," she explains.

She's hit on something important. Certain very anxious mothers are in a state of near perpetual stress. Let me go out on a limb here: why is this phenomenon so common among mothers and not fathers? Could it have something to do with social conditioning? I'd bet money on it. Immense social pressure combined with feeling almost wholly responsible for the well-being of your children is a recipe for anxiety. And this is a serious problem: by spending all their energy taking care of the children, by basically forgetting about themselves, some women see life completely pass them by. And having a partner who is open-minded and understanding isn't necessarily a game-changer. These mothers must face their fears and get out of their comfort zone; they really have to pass the puck to their partner.

Rachel Chagnon has an interesting anecdote on the subject. One of her friends came up with a unique strategy to both delegate responsibility to her partner and give herself some space: every so often she would leave him alone with the children for a week at a time, without any specific instructions, without stocking the fridge with home-cooked meals. He proved a model dad each time, taking very good care of his daughters.

"But as soon as she got home, everything fell back into its usual pattern," notes Chagnon. "In his eyes, she would take over again; he was released from the task of organizing." This example illustrates just how difficult it can be to shake up the dynamic of "captain mommy," even when she finally decides to let her partner steer.

So the division of labour is improving, but only on the surface. The logistics of everything concerning house and family still rest on women's shoulders. As Chagnon explains:

> Even when he agrees to sweep the floor and take care of meal prep every other week or do the grocery shopping, he's just following orders. He never takes responsibility for thinking about what to do, when, why, and how to do it. He's told what to do, and he does it. And he even expects a reward afterwards. Because doing these chores is a demonstration of his good intentions.[20]

This is discouraging to hear, because it's exactly what I have been noticing around me. I find the need for a reward infantilizing, no matter the form, be it flattery and pats on the back ("You're such an amazing partner!"), racking up those "Air Looses"[21] (i.e., like Air Miles) that let the partner "loose" for the Friday night hockey games with the boys, or receiving the type of positive social reinforcement that comes with putting on an apron and firing up the stove or BBQ to impress friends over the weekend. It's easy to play chef when there's no rush to whip up a nutritious meal between homework and bath every night.

I think about my girlfriends who have young children. Some work, some are at home. Most assume the thankless job of disciplining, educating, and setting limits, while their partners prefer to play with the kids. I am thinking of the ones who usually do the most demanding household chores and who, on top of everything else, are criticized for not being able to relax. I see them internalize this discourse and blame themselves, thinking that it might actually be their fault they have a hard time turning off. I can feel myself seething, like filmmaker Xavier Dolan's favourite actress Anne Dorval sitting before a completely dumbfounded TV host Richard Martineau during her brilliant 2003 invective on work-family balance for the Télé-Québec show *Les francs-tireurs*. I wanted to write this book in large part for these mothers.

Obviously, there are exceptions. Men like the ones I interviewed for this book, many of whose stories will be told later on, do exist—even if they are not representative of the vast majority of fathers—and more and more of them are showing themselves to be equal partners.

THE MYTH OF "FREE CHOICE"

The labour market was built on a model of the father-provider, someone able to devote himself entirely to his work. Family responsibilities were seen as an individual responsibility, a private matter. Since women were at home, or presumed to be at least, issues of work-family balance didn't exist, or weren't identified as such. From the moment women flooded the labour market up until the 1980s, balancing work and family was considered a woman's problem. Then, in the 1990s, employers slowly began to calculate the costs related to absenteeism, the drop in productivity, and staffing turnover due to the difficulties employees had in balancing their jobs with the demands of a family life—though we are still in the Stone Age when it comes to family accommodations for many employers.

The March 4, 2016 edition of *Le Devoir*[22] reported that "the employment rate of women with children under six is below that of men in a similar situation, although the gap has significantly narrowed in recent decades." This indicates that a gender-based division between time at work and time caring for children still persists. Even today, mothers of young children work less and opt out—temporarily or permanently—from the workforce in order to care for them.

Parenting is too often seen as an obstruction to work, a problem to contain and curb. This is why I like to borrow from Hélène Charron, Director of Research at Quebec's Council on the Status of women, who prefers to use work-family "alignment" over work-family "balance." I like this image, because it implies that the two spheres are of equal importance and must be joined together harmoniously. It pushes aside the notion of impediment, that the problem of family must be contained to keep it from hindering work efforts.

The burden of family responsibility pushes many mothers to make choices that really aren't: they choose to work in a traditionally female sector where parental obligations are more accepted or reduce their hours and refuse promotions and responsibilities that might lead to longer work days.[23] And many choose to work from home to accommodate the family. These women can kiss their own career aspirations and ambitions good-bye—moms sure know how to sacrifice!

Making women choose between having children or a career should be a thing of the past. And yet . . . If we wonder whether women can "have it all," a question that has been sparking debates between feminists for decades, the answer is no. The current trend is to say they can have it all, just not at the same time. But when I read that, all I see is a continuum of surrender that keeps changing form. It translates to the unfortunate reality that while the situation is improving, inequalities still persist.

Women still act as the home's core processor, the "control tower," to borrow from French journalist Morgane Miel.[24] In a 2015 interview aired on TFO as part of the show *Carte de visite*, former CSF president Julie Miville-Dechêne commented that:

> [W]omen don't realize gender inequalities persist until they have children. They often stop [working] longer than men, so they lose out on years of experience, career advancement, pay raises.[25]

Speaking on the same topic in October 2013 for ICI Radio-Canada Première's book program *Plus on est de fous, plus on lit!*, journalist Nathalie Collard argued, "the day men stay up at night wondering what to feed the children the next day or remembering a missed dentist appointment, that'll be the day we've achieved true equality."[26]

Without a doubt! That, and when changing tables can systematically be found in men's bathrooms—and, while we're at it, why not install the kind of "baby holders" found in public washrooms in Japan? These brilliant wall devices safely contain baby while daddy or mommy does their business.

MOTHERS AREN'T BORN, THEY'RE CREATED

Nowadays, nobody in their right mind (I'm looking at you, Doc Mailloux![27]) would say that blacks are intellectually inferior to whites. Yet when we say women are naturally more apt at caring for children because of their maternal instinct, we are engaging in the same kind of essentialist thinking.

If you are unfamiliar with the concept, essentialism argues that groups of people can be defined by objective biological characteristics that are innate and immutable. Its proponents hold that men and women are fundamentally different. Supporters of slavery championed essentialist credos to distinguish aptitudes of the black "race" from those of the white "race."

Let's clear the air once and for all, because the not-so-pretty subtext hiding behind the essentialism of innate motherhood, commonly known as "maternal instinct," is that a woman is not complete if she isn't a mother—that motherhood defines womanliness, that it's the natural role of women. Go ahead and laugh—this out-dated mentality is still widely upheld.

Women will never achieve equal opportunity as long as this archaic notion exists, since it inevitably places the burden of parental responsibility on mothers. They are confined to a stereotypical role that is both limiting and predetermined, one that is nothing but a social construct stemming from the way we raise boys to be different from girls. We foster a sense of care in the latter, spurring them to be gentle, considerate, and attentive to others' needs. We shape our girls to embody dedication and sacrifice. In a way, we are collectively "breeding" the perfect mother. Women internalize this mass cultural aliena-tion, to the point that many lack a sense of either recoil or outrage—only passivity, an acceptance of the "natural order of things." Mothers consent. They have been preparing their whole lives to perform the role that is expected of them, one through which they hope to finally gain social recognition.

YOU JANE, ME TARZAN

It isn't only women who find themselves wedged into these essentialist stereotypes. They are also harmful to men, who learn from an early age to cut themselves off from their emotions because that is what is expected of them. They become part of a culture of toxic virility, which essentially requires them to avoid appearing "weak."

In a nutshell, this culture dictates that they must be good with their hands and must never, ever cry or let slip certain so-called feminine qualities, such as being soft or gentle. Historically, men who treat their spouses with affection and enjoy caring for their children are said to be "in touch with their feminine side," something not meant to be a compliment.[28]

Yet a man can take care of children just as well as a woman can. The only biological difference is pregnancy and breastfeeding—there is nothing natural about the rest. The deep-seated myth of the innate wisdom of motherhood hurts both women, who are obviously not born with an instruction manual, and men, who feel inadequate from the outset, overwhelmed by what they believe to be their lack of "feminine intuition."

Like me, Olivier Lamalice believes that mothers are still considered the default parent and condemns the near-total lack of reflection when it comes to essentializing these roles.

> As a society, we don't ask ourselves why it's always the girls who babysit. All the parents interviewed [as part of the field research for the advisory report] talked about maternal instinct, how 'women know what to do when the baby arrives.' But when you dig further, you learn that the mother was baby-sitting by thirteen,[29] that she read all the books, consulted all the blogs and discussion groups [on parenting]. It didn't come naturally, it was training! And that's not even getting into gendered school-ing and socialization. This mother was given dolls to play with as a child. It all goes very far back.[30]

He's right, and he and I are part of the precious few "pains in the ass" asking these questions and gumming up the works. "If it ain't broke, don't fix it," he adds sarcastically.

Lamalice believes that much of awareness building can be done during prenatal classes. He argues that we can learn a lot from current train-ing courses offered to same-sex parents-to-be. "These classes focus on parenting and not just biology, childbirth, and the stages of pregnancy," he says. "We ask participants, 'What kind of parent do you want to be? How do you want to live your life?' We're looking ahead."

Interesting! Same-sex parents are non-traditional by definition; they have to question and reinvent their roles. They aren't as restricted to the long-established stereotypes as heterosexual couples are.

The CSF's 2015 report recommends that the Ministère de la Santé, the Secrétariat à la condition féminine, and the Ministère de la Famille update their prenatal classes. The Conseil wants these courses to provide unbiased information on: "the role of the parent, changes in marital relations following the arrival of a first child, the equitable division of parental leave, housework, childcare, parental responsibilities, and the economic impact of work absences, as well as include a session aimed specifically at men."

The Conseil also recommends that Quebec's public health organization, the Institut national de santé publique (INSPQ), revise the content of *From Tiny Tot to Toddler: A practical guide for parents from pregnancy to age two*, a book Quebec gives to pregnant women, to improve information on parenting roles, in particular to emphasize the importance of sharing domestic and family responsibilities. This can be done by presenting each parent's role in a non-stereotypical light and by moving the section on parenting to the beginning of the guide. It seems perfectly obvious. Because it's 2017, I want to say. We need to get our act together, and quick!

ARE STAY-AT-HOME MOMS STIGMATIZED?

I argue that women are trained for motherhood from a young age, which continues into adulthood; they hope to finally find social recognition once they become mothers. The discourse extolling motherhood is increasingly being taken up by young women—which isn't inherently negative, but some go as far as to reject feminism.

This movement reached new heights when a book entitled *Aimer, materner, jubiler*[31] (Love, Mother, Exult) by author Annie Cloutier criticized feminism for having ostracized stay-at-home moms by insisting that they must remain financially independent. It's a picture of reality that seems rather psychotronic, to say the least. Mothers didn't need to wait for feminism to emerge to feel oppressed, whether they were at home or in the workforce. Throughout history, religion, the media, and now social networks have hammered out an idealized image of mother, one that we can never measure up to. We have always made mothers feel guilty.

Rachel Chagnon agrees, recalling the emergence of hygienism[32] at the end of the 19th century and into the turn of the 20th century, "which told women that if they didn't bathe their children three times a week, they would end up killing them." At this point in our conversation, I can't help thinking of my girlfriends who make their children bathe daily and eat fruits and vegetables at every meal. If they didn't, they would feel like bad moms; as it is, they blame themselves endlessly at the slightest misstep. Some things never change!

Women still feel pressure to be perfect mothers. Just look at the wave of judgement that hit writer and columnist Geneviève Pettersen in July 2016 when she dared to write on Facebook: "parents should get a week's vacation alone to recover from time spent at home with their offspring." Outraged by all the negative comments, she wrote a pointed blog post. Here's an excerpt:

> That was all the "perfect mom squad" needed to attack my wall and rail against what I wrote. How dare I say such a thing? Because every mother has but one desire—to spend as much time as possible with her children. Complaining about my lot in life? According to the comments, maybe I should have procreated less, or not at all. Wait a second! I can't believe I'm being told I shouldn't have had children because I'm expressing a very legitimate emotion: fatigue. I'm speechless at all this social non-progress.[33]

I loved her reaction. In my opinion, it was the only way she could have responded. Many of the mothers in my circle constantly feel judged. They are afraid of not doing enough, even if, in reality, they are doing so much.

Few things make me as angry as all this guilt heaped onto mothers through blogs and social networks. As I wrote at the beginning of this chapter, the vast majority of mothers in Quebec work outside the home and are saddled with most of the domestic and family responsibilities. They're already doing everything they can, so give them a break!

But wait—there's more. The pressure to be a perfect mother is added to the unattainable beauty standards that have always been thrust on women, and it has only mutated with time. Nowadays, the perfect mother may no longer be rosy-cheeked from baking that apple pie (and yet...), but she loses the pregnancy weight overnight lest she fail to meet the ubiquitous sacrosanct model of thinness required for sex appeal and, by extension, her worth and very existence in the eyes of society.

EQUALITY IS A MYTH

IREF director Rachel Chagnon is outraged by the criticism feminists often face for disparaging stay-at-home mothers. She maintains we should never underestimate the importance of financial autonomy for women—and men, for that matter—especially if we support the Eric v. Lola court ruling on common-law spouses.[34]

Chagnon argues that we cannot both encourage women to stay home and maintain that,

> [C]ommon-law unions are every person for them-
> selves, and in the event of a separation the part-
> ners leave with what they brought to the table and
> everyone is happy. That's setting them up for fail-
> ure. It's lying. In our culture, when a couple separ-
> ates and the man wants to start a new family, he
> isn't going to take care of his ex into retirement.[35]

And I agree. We can't say it enough: under
current family law, common-law spouses, even
if they have children, are not entitled to the same
rights and responsibilities as married couples.

To remedy the situation, in June 2015 the
Family Law Advisory Committee (Comité con-
sultatif sur le droit de la famille) proposed over-
hauling the philosophy behind the Quebec family
code and imposing a mutual financial obligation
on spouses with children. Unfortunately, the
report was shelved. Chagnon continues:

> Don't forget that 70 percent of the poorest sen-
> ior citizens are women. No one's helping them
> pay their rent every month because they were
> good mothers. And I'm going to be even harsher:
> these women have children who don't have time
> to care for them. Being in a relationship doesn't
> guarantee that your life will be free of need and
> hardship. Having children doesn't guarantee it
> either. And if one day you run into financial diffi-
> culties, you won't have too many resources avail-
> able. You'll be poor, sick, and alone. And it won't
> have helped to say, "I refuse to support the femin-
> ist dogma of financial independence."[36]

Rachel Chagnon points out that most women who get behind this everyone-for-themselves attitude are frequently privileged and benefit, ironically, from a certain financial autonomy—whether they negotiated a salary from their spouse in a notarized agreement or they are financially independent through employment. And I'd add that in many cases they are married. So screw all those female common-law spouses with no safety net! Way to stick together, girls. She adds,

> You'll notice these women always thank the feminists of the past, acknowledging that they paved the way for today's freedoms and choices, while at the same time criticizing current activists for not being 'good feminists.'[37]

I'm so fed up with hearing how we've achieved equality and how feminists today take things too far!

CHAPTER 3

INVOLVED DADS: OBSTACLES AND PREJUDICE

It's a hot July afternoon, and my boyfriend and I are walking home from an outdoor city pool. We cut through the park, where they're setting up for a local festival; employees are putting together tents, fences, and an open-air stage. There is a pickup truck idling nearby (aaargh!), where I see two fairly well-built men in their late twenties or early thirties working. Heading towards us is a father on a bicycle, his daughter in the child's seat behind him. The two men call out to the father as he approaches the truck; they clearly know each other. They tease him and one attacked his manliness with a rude comment that I won't repeat. Embarrassed, the father shoots back, almost in a whisper, "Fuck off, man."

I find this anecdote speaks volumes of the independent mindedness fathers have to demonstrate even today, if they want to be involved in their children's lives—especially in certain social and professional circles. The good old macho undercurrent runs deep. But it's not that simple, even for fathers of the ambitious young professional type who we assume would have an easier time being involved in their kids' lives. Does our society approve of involved dads? I'm tempted to say that women do, but employers are a slightly different story.

In 2014, as I was planning a conference on work-family balance for officials in the Ministère des Transports and the Curateur public du Québec (transport ministry and public curator), a female acquaintance related a very telling anecdote. She was unable to pick up her sick daughter at daycare one day, so she asked her partner to do it. When he told his boss he had to leave and explained why, he was met with a visibly annoyed, "Doesn't the kid have a mother?"

Employer attitudes will change when greater numbers of fathers begin taking longer leaves after the birth of a child. Unfortunately this is still quite rare. Fathers generally limit themselves to paternity leave, taking off between three and five weeks depending on the plan they opt for. Today 85 percent take this non-transferrable leave reserved for fathers, which they lose if they fail to claim it.

It's important to note that men don't necessarily take paternity leave right after the birth.[1] Sometimes they choose to take it over the summer as if it were a kind of holiday, a paid vacation during which their role is simply to help and support the mother.

Some take things even further: one of my friends, whom I happen to be very fond of, took a week of paternity leave to go fishing with the boys. I won't name names, since he's otherwise a very involved father. But I feel this is a perfect example of how, even for the "good" dads, many still consider theirs a supporting role and not that of primary parent. And this is exactly what needs to change.

In November 2015, Facebook CEO Mark Zuckerberg announced that he would take two months of paternity leave following the birth of his daughter, explaining, "studies show that when working parents take time to be with their newborns, it's good for the entire family."

Facebook offers its US employees up to four months of paid maternity or paternity leave that they can take before the child turns one. This is an exceptionally generous program, a model program . . . for the United States anyway.

It remains well below what parents in Quebec are entitled to under the Quebec Parental Insurance Program: eighteen weeks of maternity leave, five weeks of paternity leave, and thirty-two weeks of parental leave to be shared between parents. This is the QPIP's standard plan, by far the most popular among Quebecers. The QPIP also offers a shorter plan with higher benefits that includes three weeks of paternity leave, fifteen weeks of maternity leave, and twenty-five weeks of parental leave.

And yet two months of paternity leave is much more than the vast majority of Quebec fathers take, who generally limit themselves to the five weeks' paternity leave or less. Zuckerberg, who heads one of the world's largest companies in a country where conditions for working mothers are far from rosy, has certainly contributed to changing mindsets in the business community regarding the importance of leave-taking for parents, both in the United States and in Quebec. He is sending a powerful and crucial message.

Even in Quebec, taking paternity leave is still frowned upon. One out of every three male employees in Quebec believes that if a father takes leave when a child is born, his employer won't be happy. And half of men think that taking paternity leave could hurt their career. These are the results of a November 2015 employee survey conducted by Quebec's human resources association, the Ordre des conseillers en ressources humaines agréés du Québec.

In a government document celebrating the ten-year anniversary of the QPIP,[2] doctor of economics and human resources specialist Diane Gabrielle Tremblay writes:

> Our research on fathers shows that great progress has been made over the past twelve years. That being said, men who have resolved to embrace

fatherhood may face challenges. Resistance in the workplace, often stemming from the employer but in some cases from colleagues, may curb their desire. . . . Employer resistance can take different forms. Fathers have reported being asked to move their weeks off to a slower period for the company or to shorten them. In certain cases an employer might ask a father to give up his share of parental leave and take only paternity leave, which they see as being sufficient. Some employers may even call or email fathers while they are out on paternity leave and ask them to do a bit of work or, at the very least, monitor their files while they are gone. Some fathers have worked a few hours or even full days here and there while on leave. Some reported having worked an average of one day a week, and many found themselves discussing work when they stopped by to introduce the new baby to colleagues! . . . Our research shows that as a rule, women are rarely disturbed during their leave.

This clearly illustrates the persistent double standard wherein fathers, unlike mothers, cannot fully assume their role as parent.

In 2016, two cases of discrimination against new fathers out on parental leave caught my eye, since they both confirm concerns expressed in the survey. The first was widely publicized in April 2016. A man who managed a restaurant in the Quebec City area filed a complaint with the health, safety and equity board, the CNESST, against his former employer because he was dismissed the day after filing for paternity leave.[3]

I hope he wins the case and that the ruling makes big waves. It is vital for men to be able to become more involved as parents.

The second case involves the partner of an elected city official who prefers to remain anonymous. He had been working for a community organization for six years. This wasn't Standard and Poor's—he worked in the non-profit sector and received an excellent performance evaluation every year.

His wife's second pregnancy fell in the middle of her term in office and since she was not entitled to any leave,[4] he decided to take the complete thirty-two week parental leave. He notified his employer when his spouse was three months pregnant. The employer made derogatory comments as if in jest, saying that he never thought he'd be faced with such a situation coming from a male employee.

Two months later, the man received a surprise evaluation that proved devastatingly negative. It stated that the situation was serious in all areas of performance, and that if things did not improve the employer would have to dismiss him. This man rejected the evaluation and demanded justification. The board of directors withdrew it, stammering that they had no concrete examples of poor performances, only impressions. Then the employee went on parental leave for eight months.

One month before coming back to work, he received a letter from the board notifying him that his position had been re-evaluated and modified; instead of thirty-five hours a week, Monday to Friday from nine to five, it had been reduced to twenty-six hours a week, including three night shifts minimum and a full day Saturday. With a partner in office and two young children at home, it was obviously impossible for him to meet the new conditions. He was forced to resign, forfeiting eligibility for unemployment benefits.

When I think about his case, I see both blatant discrimination against the father and, more globally, an affront to all working mothers. Clearly the takeaway is that men should not be doing the parenting, since that is a woman's domain.

As noted in the first chapter, it seems we punish working women who have children based on the insidious notion that their place is in the home, rearing children, and we punish fathers who want to go against the grain so they understand it isn't a man's role. A leopard can't change its spots: the traditional father-breadwinner/mother-homemaker model isn't going anywhere. Talk about appalling attitudes that are deeply entrenched!

INVOLVED DAD, REJECTED DAD?

Jean-Philippe Pleau, devoted, modern, and egalitarian father of two school-aged girls and a baby boy, is a producer at ICI Radio-Canada Première (CBC) and co-hosts its show *C'est fou*.

On International Women's Day, March 8, 2016, he posted the following Facebook status:

> Have no fear, *my daughters' school* (CSDM's École Saint-Fabien) is not making little feminists out of them. Here are a few choice sentences my youngest is reading about parents.
>
> 1) Dad works a lot at the office.
> 2) Dad made a bonfire by the beach.
> 3) Emma is queen of winter carnival.
> 4) Dad goes to watch Jules at the ice rink.
> 5) Mom peels vegetables.
> 6) Dad goes fishing with Charlie.
> 7) Mom put my socks into the washing machine.
>
> Happy Women's Day everyone!

Pleau has a background in sociology and believes that even beyond individual reflexes, our entire system fuels these representations. "We're stuck in the day-to-day, and we don't even stop to think," he says. After a few similar experiences, he decided to act. As he put it, "It had gotten out of hand—it was too much." So he met with his daughter's teacher, who hadn't noticed the sexist nature of the sentences Pleau singled out in his March 8 Facebook status. "She said she would address it," he adds. "I don't think she intended to place women in the home or relegate them to that role, but these sentences aren't innocuous."

This isn't the first time Pleau has ranted about parenthood issues. In 2015, he signed an open letter in *Le Devoir* entitled "Vivre sa paternité dans la dignité" (Living a dignified paternity).[5] This article spurred me to interview Pleau for this book. I think it's a real gem that deserves an excerpt here (with permission from the author!):

> A father's role has changed a lot over the past forty years in Quebec. We owe this progress in large part to feminism, to fathers' collective desire to shatter the provider-husband/absent father image and also, in recent years, to a political will resulting in the establishment of a paternity leave worthy of its name, though there is still room for improvement.
>
> Ten years ago, I was finishing a master's degree in sociology at the Université Laval, writing a dissertation on work-family balance for young fathers entitled *Services manquants, pères manqués?* (Missing services, or forgotten fathers?) The research question was simple: do services offered to parents and their application across Quebec take fathers into consideration, too? At the time, I concluded that there was very little evidence. . . .
>
> Words are never just words. They have power, they are power. Take, for instance, a recent episode in the gym at my daughters' school. . . . As the activity was winding down, a teacher brought all the children in the room together and said, "Raise your hand if your mother isn't here. If your mother didn't come today, you'll go to the after-school program. If your mother is here, you can leave with her."
>
> By my most honest estimate, there were roughly as many mothers as fathers in the gym that day. As I have been doing on a regular basis for the past three years at these types of school events, I raised my hand, pointed out that there were several dads

in the room, and suggested she use a wording that reflected the reality. It earned me an eye roll. So be it.

But just then, a puzzled kindergartener raised his hand and asked, "What do I do if my dad is here?" This isn't insignificant. This little boy wondered what he should do since his father had attended the activity and not his mother.

We know that social construction of gender is a process that begins very early on, and it is likely that this child's brain will encode, or "socially reproduce" as Pierre Bourdieu would say, the following: in the eyes of the school, a very influential agent of socialization, the parent who should attend this type of activity is the mother.

Seated in the Radio-Canada cafeteria between recording sessions, Pleau continues:

What struck me the most was the reaction of this little boy who came from a same-sex family and had two dads. . . . He was completely lost, and he perfectly illustrated our own incomprehension. But the other dads and I didn't mention it again. Everything goes so quickly, we can't question it all. Unless something clearly crosses a line, only then do we say, "OK, that really goes against my personal values."[6]

He addresses gender stereotypes that abound in children's literature. I ask him why it's still an issue today. Why haven't things changed? "It seems like society hasn't adjusted to the reality. Things still exist, even if we haven't labelled them correctly. A centre called *mère-enfant*[7] (mother-child) doesn't mean fathers don't use it."

When he was expecting a child and called the centre to ask if he could come in, not only did the receptionist answer in a self-evident tone, but she didn't even understand why he would ask the question. "It was as if the words held no weight," he continues. "But if I'm hungry, I'm more likely to search for *restaurant*, not *garage*. The designation should match the services offered."

ENDING THE GHETTOISATION OF WOMEN

Work-family balance should no longer be considered a female-specific issue to be addressed only by feminists, argues Jean-Philippe Pleau. He believes it concerns everyone, and that reformulating the issue would be unifying and facilitate father involvement. With three children who have two different mothers, he has experience with joint custody and is always stumbling over work-family balance and school. In May 2016, he posted another Facebook status on the subject:

> Though I've had joint custody for years and today was my day with the kids, the school once again called only their mother to say my daughter was sick.
> The result: since they couldn't reach Mom, no one came to pick her up!
> For the first two years, the school didn't even send me paperwork," he tells me. "And since I wasn't on very good terms with their mother at the time, if the school didn't give me the information I wouldn't get it at all. I kept telling them, "I don't

want to give you extra work, but society is evolving and we're beyond this." It took me two years to get the information, a second folder, and duplicate photocopies. It's mind-boggling![8]

In light of his experience, I wonder why there is this apparent resistance to social change, why schools are having difficulty adapting to the fact that some fathers are becoming more involved with their children. I feel they should be welcomed enthusiastically and included without reservation. As a society, we have everything to gain from sharing the mental load and responsibilities equally between parents.

Since schools have a large proportion of female employees and are highly unionized, it seems to me they should be fertile ground for social progressivism and feminism. So why are they finding it difficult to involve fathers? Clearly, the idea that Mom is the primary parent, explored in the second chapter, is as deeply rooted in schools as it is in the rest of society.

GUYS' REALM, GIRLS' REALM

I repeat, as long as the mother is considered the primary parent by default, we will never achieve equality. And the fact that to this day our school systems, particularly the primary schools, are almost exclusively female is symptomatic of the problem. It all reflects persistent stereotypes about gender identity that need to be dismantled.

Christine Fréchette, director of Public Affairs and External Relations at Montréal International, is a long-time feminist activist. Among other things, she was instrumental in helping create a parental leave program in Quebec worthy of its name. She denounces prohibitive stereotypes, such as prejudices against men working in traditionally female-dominated fields like teachers and daycare workers, which can be considered a logical extension of the feminization of childcare:

> I was shocked to hear that guys who work in CPEs (daycares) were questioned about their motives. . . . I knew three such men who all left the profession because they were fed up with having to justify themselves, even though it was a profession they were truly passionate about. Prejudice and barriers still exist, mainly because we have yet to question the traditional roles attributed to men in the same way we've done with women. What new model have we created for them? They've had to do it themselves, since socially speaking we haven't developed the tools to encourage them to think outside the box, as we have done with women. For instance, the competition Hat's Off to You![9] encourages diversity in [girls'] education choices.[10]

I agree with Fréchette that there is a shortage of men in the education and childcare sectors. Just as they should be considered equal caregivers, men should be able to work in childcare, a sector traditionally associated with women, without their sacrosanct virility being called into question.

On a side note: it would be great for women to be able to access traditionally male-dominated sectors, too. But they can barely get through the door, blocked during the hiring process. And the few who do manage to get a foot in are frequently the victims of intimidation. The excellent documentary *Casques roses*[11] portrays the extent of discrimination against women working in the construction industry. And in other traditionally male-dominated—I'd go so far as to say chauvinistic— fields, such as information technology and engineering, let's just say that for women, the battle has only just begun.[12]

SWIMMING AGAINST THE CURRENT

Laurent Turcot is a Canada Research Chair and history professor at the Université du Québec à Trois-Rivières. He has two children with his spouse, who works full-time outside the home. He mainly works from home and has a very flexible schedule. Every morning around six he wakes the children and fixes them breakfast while his partner takes a shower and gets ready. Then he drops her off at work, brings the children to daycare, and comes home to eat breakfast and start his workday.

> I have an unusual job. I could work morning, noon, night, and weekends if I wanted to, but I have an agreement with my girlfriend. If I were like my col-

leagues, I'd be going to conferences all around the world each month. But I don't feel like I'm missing out. And my girlfriend carried three children [she suffered a miscarriage], spent twenty-six months of her life pregnant and more than two years at home. That's a total of four years she lost in the workforce. That's why I do a lot.[13]

Laurent Turcot considers the parenthood problem a cultural issue:

The fact that it's always the mother who takes parental leave, that I'm a UFO when I take care of my children, that everyone in the neighbourhood asks me where their mother is proves that we haven't achieved equality. Many people see the fact that I'm a stay-at-home dad[14] as a symbolic castration.

Both realistic and honest, Turcot doesn't balk at addressing the private reality of inequality—the aforementioned invisible labour that still rests almost entirely on mothers' shoulders:

My girlfriend is the foundation of our home, I'm just the walls. She does all the planning, while I do most of the visible stuff on a daily basis. But without her, everything would crumble.

To illustrate his point, he mentions the time he took his sick daughter to the clinic and the doctor—a woman!—told him, "Your spouse is a lucky woman!"

> At the time, it made me really happy. I was like, "Damn, I'm awesome!" But when I got home, I asked my girlfriend, "Would anyone say that to you?"

This anecdote brilliantly illustrates the double standard of expectations for fathers and mothers. A woman taking her sick child to the doctor is just business as usual.

While the doctor's reaction is positive reinforcement for the father, it also illustrates how rarely these duties fall to someone other than the mother.

> When I told her, she was furious; she feels guilty when she's not with the kids. The moment something's up, it's, "Daddy, Daddy, Daddy," not like what we learned—that children are naturally drawn to the mother.[15]

Though it's 2018, the message that gets drilled in is still "Mom knows bet." This is why some women gush when fathers get involved—they see it as exceptional.

In contrast, men will question the masculinity of fathers who are involved with caring for their children—to the extent that some feel entitled to disparage them, even to their face, and even when they are clients! Here's what happened to Jean-Philippe Pleau:

> This week I worked from home because someone was supposed to come by and install an alarm

system. When he arrived, I was doing the dishes. We sat down at the table with him, a man in his forties, my partner, and me, and I took the baby. He said something rude like, "Oh, she had you do the housework and take care of the baby today—what a lucky lady." It was ridiculous, because I do the dishes almost 100 percent of the time and the baby is naturally 50-50. I felt like saying, "Where do you get off thinking like that?!"

I couldn't help saying that in my opinion there are legions of guys like this and that Pleau is the exception. But I like his surprise. I like that he is astonished by the prevailing sexism. Perhaps, like his rapper friend Koriass, he is a "Natural Born Féministe."[16]

IS DIVISION OF LABOUR NATURAL?

Jean-Philippe Pleau also brings up the issue of invisible labour, addressed earlier with Olivier Lamalice. Pleau estimates that he spends thirty to forty minutes a day meal planning and shopping:

> It could happen in the metro and no one would know. In my circle of friends, even if at first glance it seems like a traditional division of labour, a lot of people I know choose tasks according to their interests and availabilities. And it works. It doesn't mean that there's no room for improvement, but already it's good to discuss and offer to do the things we prefer.[17]

I have my own doubts about this idea of preference. My own relationship is very traditional: my partner wields the hammer, as his father did before him, and I enjoy cooking, something I watched my mother do as a child. But aren't these pseudo-"preferred interests"—just behavioural reproductions resulting from the gendered socialization and upbringing we experienced? I'd say they definitely are.

I grew up in the 1980s and still have wonderful memories of the Christmas catalogue put out by a certain department store I won't name. My brother, sister, and I used to drool over the pages full of toys. The pink pages for girls advertised dolls, kitchenettes, mini ironing boards, play microwave ovens, and other baking sets that came with a little recipe book. The boy pages included a plastic toolbox like Dad's, play workbenches, and lots of trucks. In both cases, we were taught from a young age which activities were gender-appropriate.

And it's not like things have changed. More than ever, mothers around me complain about gendered marketing, pink for girls and blue for boys, making a comeback in recent years. But beyond the toys, I can see that we still transmit gendered parenting roles. Many families pass on inequities when it comes to dividing up household chores, and children simply mimic them.

Towards my later teenage years, my older brother and younger sister and I lived with my mother and her boyfriend. Every week my mother would make a list of household chores for us and tape it to the refrigerator. My sister and I did them obediently while my brother weaseled his way out, giggling and turning up his nose at these demeaning tasks. And he got away with it all the time. He'd never even lift a finger, because deep down we all agreed, consciously or not, that cleaning is women's work. In light of Olivier Lamalice's field study, I'm not so sure things have changed all that much.

FOR A TRULY INVOLVED DAD

While writing the 2015 CSF woman's status board report on sharing parental leave, Lamalice conducted individual interviews with numerous parent couples from all different socioeconomic backgrounds. In each case, he noted an obvious contradiction between theory and practice when it came to parental equality. This is why he advocates for better division of parental leave.

> Foreign studies and experiences tend to show that the more fathers are involved earlier in their children's lives, the greater the positive impact on interpersonal relationships. Everyone agrees. The more present the parent, the closer he or she is to the child. It's pretty much common knowledge. But the more time the father spends at home, the more he'll realize what a huge job it is, the household chores as well as childcare. Because it's easy to

gloss over things when we don't exactly know how they get done.[18]

When he conducted interviews with parent couples as part of his research, he asked them to describe three routines—morning, after school/work, and bedtime. Fathers tended to describe their role in detail while summing up their partners' involvement. "They would say, 'My girlfriend washes the dishes and does bedtime,'" he tells me.

By being there, by being the only parent at home, by performing these tasks and realizing what they entail, the father finally understood that doing the dishes, making dinner, or putting the kid to bed isn't just one action—it's like seventy-two thousand actions, one after the other, by the time you're finished. And that, obviously, pushes them to be more involved.[19]

In the report written in collaboration with Hélène Charron, Lamalice writes that:

[E]ven when parents reorganize the division of labour, the fathers generally continue to perform less housework. But as soon as they take on a few new tasks, mothers tend to claim that the new division is even. One mother reported, "Now he does the bath while I do the dishes, he does the shopping while I do the cleaning; it's really 50-50." Yet later in the interview we learn that the mother does all the housework, the laundry, the dusting, in addition to caring for the child, with the exception of bath time.[20]

I ask why he believes the fathers interviewed were so keen to highlight their contributions and tended to downplay the importance of their spouse's responsibilities.

> I don't think it's conscious, but it's not all that unrelated to the perceived differentiation of tasks. First, there's the principle of separation, in which there are male chores and female chores. And then there's the principle of hierarchy, where men's tasks are more important than women's tasks.[21]

I point out how the private sphere mimics the labour market, since traditionally masculine jobs are the most valued and the best paid. He agrees, adding that when a profession becomes feminized it loses value. "In the past, the director of human resources was very important to a company," he notes. "But it lost its appeal and prestige as it was feminized."

He comes back to the principle of separation. "We are socialized this way; it's much more important to say, 'I'm going to renovate' or 'I'm going to build a shed' than 'I'm going to take care of my child.'" I tell him I suspect that even women have internalized this mindset. He couldn't agree more. He adds,

> And it's reflected in the job market. We frequently hear that it's normal for a male construction worker to earn more than a female daycare worker. Why is that? If working on a construction site requires

certain skills, I bet the same goes for educating children.[22]

I remind him sarcastically that everyone knows these skills are innate to women, that they come naturally, no effort required.

The fathers cited in Lamalice's report see themselves as helpers, awaiting instructions from the boss-mom:

> It's our first child, and she took on a lot. She could have given me some chores, but I practically had to fight to get them. In the end, she never gave me jobs to do. I would have liked to do more, not necessarily because I enjoy cleaning, but so she wouldn't have been so tired.[23]

Not only does he not "help" his spouse (in other words, do his share of the home and family upkeep), but he also seems incapable of taking the smallest initiative, preferring to wait for tasks to be delegated to him. The mother wound up with the burden all on her shoulders.

And the cherry on top: the father then starts complaining that his spouse is always tired, suggesting that it isn't his fault she can't delegate. That's taking it too far! I'm almost tempted to send this man the definition of the word *initiative*, since he appears to be unfamiliar with it. Who knows? It might lead to a revelation. It couldn't hurt.

All kidding aside, Lamalice advocates for a longer paternity leave to solve the labour division imbalance that plagues parents. Accounts of fathers who have shared the parental leave have proven that this would be an effective solution. Their testimonies appear in the CSF report:

> When I stayed home, I realized just how unfair the division of labour can be. It's easy to see the dishes that need doing, to close your eyes, and just leave them there. And in the end, it's always the same person who clears them up.

> When it's five weeks, you see it like a big vacation. You visit with family, you don't spend much time at home. But four months really showed me what it's like to stay home . . . holy cow!

> By being home more often, I realize how hard it is to get things done with three children around. It's clear that the more time you spend with the kids, the less you have for household chores.[24]

WHEN DAD BECOMES THE "LEAD PARENT"

Andrew Moravcsik is married to Anne-Marie Slaughter, well-known author of the 2012 article "Why Women Still Can't Have It All,"[25] that she published with *The Atlantic* while working under Secretary of State Hillary Clinton. In a long piece also published in *The Atlantic*, this time in October 2015,[26] Moravcsik writes about his experience as a self-employed dad and "lead parent."

> For men, lead parenting can also be lonely. Parent networks are essential for raising children. They

transmit crucial information—about good and bad teachers, carpooling, extracurricular activities, summer camps, and much else. These networks tend to be dominated by moms who understandably invest a lot in them socially. At school events, the moms gossip with each other and make plans; I get out my laptop and try to catch up on work.

He writes that "cultural barriers to male lead parenting only grow stronger as children—and parents—age. A dad in his twenties or thirties who takes some time off to care for an infant is adorable," but is less so the older he becomes. Andrew Moravcsik addresses the notion of ageism, which he argues also affects fathers. He notes that an older man who limits his work schedule or professional ambition to attend to a teenager is to be "suspect," that he has no ambition.

This brings us back to the beginning of the chapter. Society values men who are involved parents, but not too involved. Taking baby for a walk in the stroller is charming, but taking thirty-two weeks of parental leave—let's not get carried away!

Andrew Moravcsik paints a gloomy picture of male parenthood. He argues that while Generation Y men hope for more egalitarian marriages, a lack of opportunities for work-life balance in full-time employment forces them to reproduce traditional roles. "Both sexes are trapped in the same system, which has defined a one-dimensional role for each."

He calls to end gendered stereotyping, which keeps mothers at home and fathers distanced from the family sphere. He writes of his own experience at home in a very positive light, arguing that by becoming lead parents "men can get what many moms have long had—a very close relationship with their kids."

Many mothers I know would agree. One confided that the father of her daughters was very close to the older one because he was unemployed when she was born, while the mother had needed to return to work quickly. This was well before the Quebec Parental Insurance Program came into effect. Her partner took care of their daughter for the first year of her life. Of course he loves both his daughters, but he seems to have a stronger and much closer bond with the eldest. Consider this my plea for a better division of parental leave, one that encourages fathers to be more present in the first months of a child's life. This is the issue I will address in the next chapter.

CHAPTER 4

SHARING PARENTAL LEAVE— A RADICAL STEP?

I met Christine Fréchette one beautiful June morning to discuss her role in developing a better public parental insurance plan in Quebec.[1] It all began in 1999, just after she had given birth. Parental leave was six months at the time, administered by the federal government through employment insurance. As a young activist, Fréchette kept a close eye on the negotiations between Quebec and Ottawa over repatriating the funds—negotiations that would eventually stretch over seven years.

At that time, the notion of a non-transferable paternity leave didn't exist. There was maternity leave for the mother, and the rest of the parental leave could be shared between parents. The mother took it in 93 percent of cases, for all sorts of reasons— she may have earned less, or since she was already on leave, she just continued staying home with the baby. Fathers often began putting in overtime after the birth to make up for the loss of the woman's wages.[2]

What convinced her to advocate for a father-only leave came during her time as a member of Quebec's status of women board, the CSF—Fréchette served nine years in total on the 10-member board—when she learned about the situation in Norway:

> They'd instituted a non-transferrable paternity leave that completely changed things. That was when I decided we had to do the same in Quebec, that we were progressive enough when it came to feminist and parental issues to make it happen.[3]

She convinced other members of the CSF board to support the measure and advertise it publicly.

> At the same time, I was working with my partner and friends to set up what we called the *mouvement des bébés du millénaire* (millennial baby movement) that united young parents advocating for the government of Quebec's bid to repatriate management of the parental insurance fund. We wanted to show that there was public support. We organized a press conference and a stroller parade down Boulevard Saint-Laurent.[4]

The movement promoted the idea that self-employed workers should be entitled to parental leave benefits. "Especially since freelancing was becoming more popular with the younger generations and social programs should reflect workplace trends," notes Fréchette. "But the group's primary goal was to bring the idea of a non-transferrable paternity leave to Quebec. We drafted a statement and collected a hundred signatures in under two weeks, then brought it before a parliamentary committee."

> We were told that it was an innovative approach. So they listened, in part because we'd gone off the beaten path, honestly. They asked how we'd been able to mobilize so quickly, but the moment people read our statement they were eager to sign. Things had reached that point.[5]

Fréchette believes the movement achieved its goals through the creation of the Quebec Parental Insurance Program, which gave self-employed workers access to benefits and established a separate paternity leave, even though not all of its suggestions were retained. For example, the movement advocated for a ten- to twelve-week paternity leave, fearing a shorter leave would be seen as a symbolic gesture. However, some members of the parliamentary committee felt that such a long leave for the father would punish the mother.

Determined to remain optimistic, Fréchette believed things would nevertheless improve with the institution of a non-transferrable five-week paternity leave:

I said, "They [fathers] are going to try it out, like it, and understand why this leave is so important." I also thought it would have an impact on the workplace, that men would better understand women when they explained to their colleagues and bosses that they'd be taking time off, not to go on vacation but to take care of the baby. It was so that women wouldn't be the only ones to be labelled 'parental leave risk.' Now men would join them—to a lesser extent, sure, but still. It puts the wheels in motion. After taking off for a birth, a father should be completely justified in taking off for a sick child.[6]

But Fréchette insists on one thing: paternity leave shouldn't simply replace the mother-in-law who traditionally came to help during the lying-in period.

The mother obviously plays a critical role during the first days, weeks, and months following the birth. But the father shouldn't only be there for support. When the father spends time at home alone with the child, it makes him a better caregiver. Being close to the baby helps him assume parental responsibilities, understand the dynamic, and become part of the family unit.[7]

A recent article[8] summarizing sociologist Erin Rehel's 2012-13 study on changing perceptions of fatherhood, masculinity, and paternity leave across Canada and the United States reinforces the view Fréchette and I share:

A policy enabling mothers and fathers to experience a similar transition to parenthood has tremendous potential to bring about a more gender-equitable division of childcare in heterosexual couples, even once paternity leave ends. This longer leave challenges women's supposedly innate superior parenting skills by giving men time for analogous experiences; being released from professional responsibilities allows them to fully commit to parenthood. It encourages fathers to make the shift from a supporting role to that of co-parent, an observation in line with research that demonstrates a father's early and continuous participation in childrearing leads to greater longterm involvement.

But couples still have to agree to share their parental leave. Taking off five weeks for paternity leave is great, but is being gone six, seven, or eight months still as cool? Are men willing to make this sacrifice, to put their careers on the back burner—like women do—and take on more of the parental leave?

TRANSFERRABLE LEAVE THAT'S RARELY TRANSFERRED

Quebec is a trailblazer in North America when it comes to paternity leave, borrowing from a tried-and-true template popular in Scandinavian nations. A three- to five-week paternity leave in Quebec, depending on the plan, lets beneficiaries receive up to 75 percent of their salary. It's certainly easy to see why 80 percent of new fathers take advantage of the policy.

Yet fathers in Quebec are more hesitant when it comes to the transferrable leave. And they are not alone. The Organisation for Economic Co-Operation and Development (OECD) recently announced that parental leave is still unequally distributed between men and women in countries where it exists.[9]

In its April 2015 report, the CSF argues that "the current challenge is not to convince new fathers to take the leave reserved for them; it is to achieve a more equitable six- to eight-month parental leave."

The fact remains that only 35 percent of new fathers in Quebec take even a small portion of this transferrable parental leave. And the few who do are not away from work for long. In 2010, among the 30 percent of fathers who claimed parental leave, a quarter took just an additional week or two on top of their paternity leave. At the other end of the spectrum, only slightly more than 30 percent took between nine and thirty-two weeks. And I'd bet we're talking closer to nine weeks than thirty-two.[10]

Nonetheless, we have made progress: until the QPIP was introduced, fathers were only allowed five days off! Yet mothers are still overwhelmingly perceived as the primary parent, while fathers see themselves in a supporting role, an impression confirmed by two surveys conducted by Léger Marketing in 2011 and Zins Beauchesne and Associates in 2014.[11] In both cases, almost two thirds of fathers interviewed said they wanted to support the mother by taking a leave of absence, thereby defining their role as supporting that of the mother.

And before we build a shrine to fathers who take part of the parental leave, it should be noted that in the vast majority of cases[12] these fathers do so because the mother is ineligible (unemployed, studying, on sick leave, a claimant with the CNESST (health and safety board)). And in more than 80 percent of cases, mothers are at home while fathers are on parental leave. As a result, these men never find themselves in the role of sole caregiver.[13]

FEAR OF CHANGE

In the spring of 2015, I noted with interest that France changed its parental leave policy in favour of a successive, rather than concomitant,[14] leave to be shared equally between parents. The idea was to sharpen the father's parental skills and reflexes. It sounded revolutionary.

At about the same time, the CSF announced a more modest proposal aiming to reinforce the father-child bond and encourage men to take on a greater share of parenting responsibilities. Reserving three weeks of parental leave for the exclusive use of fathers, argued the CSF, was a way to extend paternity leave and reduce the transferrable parental leave by as much. The proposal was at zero cost and would not require additional funding to the program.

While not as bold as France's proposal, the CSF proposal nevertheless elicited indignant reactions. First from women who felt stripped of what should be their right. Then from people—I'll come back to this—who were quick to argue that the state had no business interfering in citizens' private lives. As if the government's role isn't to change societal perceptions by implementing concrete measures that challenge systemic discrimination!

Lots of government decisions geared towards gender equality and the common good have had a positive effect on our society: establishing the Ministry of Education and making education compulsory to sixteen, instituting Family Patrimony, creating the CPE (daycare) system or the *Pay Equity Act* (though things are far from perfect). These so-called "intrusions" into citizens' private lives have led to social progress and propelled us forward in terms of equality.

IS QUEBEC LATE TO THE GAME?

Quebec's parental leave plan may be blazing trails for equality across North America, but it still lags behind many countries in Europe and Scandinavia.

In 2016, Iceland proposed a system I find to be remarkably innovative. The total parental leave is set at twelve months, with five reserved for the mother, five reserved for the father, and two to be shared between parents. Now there's a progressive public policy fostering equality between working men and women! Sexist hiring practices would be a thing of the past if men were granted nearly the same length of parental leave.

In Germany, paternity leave is two months, in Belgium, four. Under the Norwegian model, fathers take a mandatory two-week paternity leave once the child is born—an excellent idea, in my opinion—and the remaining parental leave reserves ten weeks for their exclusive use. In Sweden, a father is entitled to twelve weeks of leave. These countries all offer more attractive programs than Quebec's current five-week model. Longer non-transferrable leaves reinforce a father's role and involvement and encourage a more equitable division of family responsibilities in the long term. But while Sweden is frequently cited as a model system, it shouldn't be regarded as a paragon of equality. Remember that Swedish men only take 20 percent of the transferrable leave to which they are entitled. Still, Quebec is far behind by comparison.

Well aware of parenthood's persistent inequalities, certain governments have improved programs aimed at new parents. In 2016, the Conseil de gestion de l'assurance parentale published a report that noted:

[S]ome countries encourage parents to divide their leave equally by adding supplemental payouts when it is shared evenly between mother and father. Sweden is a prime example, instituting a bonus for gender equality. Germany will extend parental leave by two months if the father takes a leave of absence for at least this long. Japan subscribes to a similar approach, adding two months of benefits when both parents take leave.

FRANCE'S ATTEMPT AT EQUALITY

With its longstanding reputation for machismo, France made big waves with its January 2015 policy: paternity leave now stands at six months. The reform was part of the *Loi pour l'égalité réelle entre les femmes et les hommes* (Act for Real Equality between Women and Men), which includes provisions for equal access to professional responsibilities and sports, violence against women, and political parity.

The reform's stated goal is an equal division of parental leave for a couple's first child: six months' maternity leave, followed by six months' paternity leave. Before the reform, parental leave consisted of a total of six months, taken by mothers in the vast majority of cases, while paternity leave matched Quebec's five-week policy. The new program doesn't take anything away from mothers—rather, it doubles the initial parental leave, provided the supplementary six months are taken exclusively by the father before the child is eighteen months old.

In France, the duration of parental leave is extended for a second or third child; this pre-reform policy remains unchanged. There is a three-year leave for a second or third child, provided the father takes six months. If he doesn't, the leave drops to two and a half years.

The government hopes to tackle an imbalance in parental responsibilities and keep mothers in the workforce with its policy. The symbolic gesture is loud and clear—*symbolic,* since the income replacement benefits are a paltry $550 per month and cannot be combined if both parents take leave at the same time. As a result, theory did not translate to practice and the status quo persists: mothers take the entirety of the parental leave, with men only accounting for 4 percent of parents who take leave.

It's all well and good to send a strong message, but we must be equipped to make concrete changes. Nevertheless, it indicates that sharing parental responsibilities is a sign of the times, making headway across Europe and Canada.

While benefits offered in France are well below those granted by the Quebec program, Quebec could stand to gain by France's position of furthering the idea that parental leave need not be a woman's exclusive domain.

It was discouraging to witness the media's skeptical reaction to the CSF recommendation of three weeks' parental leave reserved for the father. I realized just how far we have to go, and how implementing measures promoting equality in parenthood will be an uphill battle. This resistance to change is indicative of the true evolution of mores in our so-called "progressive" society.

WHAT A JOKE...

Although the French reform made barely a ripple in Quebec, the few reactions it did provoke were negative. I was outraged to read comments in *Les affaires* from Florent Francoeur, CEO of the CRHA, Quebec's human resources professionals association. Asked whether Quebec would benefit from France's parental leave system he retorted, "If it's not broke, don't fix it."[15] Later in the article he claims that fathers are already doing their fair share since "the vast majority of Quebecers take their five-week paternity leave and a third of those take additional parental leave."[16]

So according to the CEO of the CRHA, everything is under control; dads are doing their part. Seriously? If 80 percent of fathers take the exclusive paternity leave and only a third of those take a share—often a minimal one—of the parental leave, we're sitting pretty? Long live the status quo? I'm sorry, but parenting responsibilities are still far from equal! With lower thresholds for involvement, declaring fathers already do their fair share is like saying it's normal and acceptable—even natural and desirable—for mothers to take on more.

And the worst part is that it's a global issue, as indicated by the OECD study cited above. Though paid parental leave exists in twenty-three of the twenty-four member countries, it is still largely utilized by women. And *that's* the crux of the matter. So how can we change it? How can we stop parenthood from being an exclusively female responsibility so that mothers can thrive professionally?

The study also concludes, corroborating data from Léger Marketing, that fathers are hesitant to take parental leave because they fear their careers will suffer. But do you think women aren't worried about the negative impact parental leave could have on their career? Should it always fall to them to make these sacrifices and pay the price?

Why not aim for equality? The idea obviously isn't to penalize both men and women for procreating; we need to permanently change perceptions so that having children is seen as a positive thing. Let's give a hand to those brave enough to start a family, for goodness sake! In Finland, the number of men who took parental leave doubled between 2006 and 2013. We can get there, too!

Without claiming that fathers are pulling their weight and the status quo is working out great, as Florent Francoeur would have us believe, let's acknowledge that the QPIP is a step in the right direction. But we can't forget there's work to be done, that the current system doesn't do enough to check discriminatory hiring practices and sexism in the workplace for mothers and women of child-bearing age, depriving them of equal opportunity and ambitions.

It's infuriating to hear this kind of economic discourse coming from a human resources expert; he's completely overlooking systemic maternity-related discrimination in the work-force. It echoes the reception the CSF proposal garnered in 2015.

It came as no surprise when Yves-Thomas Dorval, CEO of the Quebec's business lobby, the Conseil du patronat du Québec, declared on a Radio-Canada radio show [17] that it wasn't the role of the state to interfere in people's private lives, that it was a question of personal choice, just has he argued that women now earn as much, if not more than their husbands[18]—contrary to every statistic available on the subject—, and that it should be up to the couple to decide. Could he be more out of touch with reality?

The fact that mothers are the ones taking par-ental "leave" in the majority of cases isn't always a choice; as we've seen, the dominant essentialist ideology still plagues women with guilt and places them in the role of "control tower" responsible for maintaining the domestic sphere. Francoeur and Dorval base their arguments on the assumption that we have attained gender equality; however, we know this is simply not the case.

You might have noticed that I put the word *leave* in quotation marks above. The term irritates me, to be honest. For the love of God, we're not talking about a holiday! It may be a leave from work, but looking after a child under twenty-four months is extremely demanding. It's what feminists call women's *invisible work*. In the 1970s, the debate over paying stay-at-home moms a salary almost tore feminists apart. And from time to time, the issue still resurfaces. The title of a play by the Théâtre des cuisines borrowed from an Yvon Deschamps monologue sums it up best: *Môman travaille pas, a trop d'ouvrage!* (Mom doesn't work, she's got too much to do!)[19]

Olivier Lamalice thinks fathers become more aware of the workload that caring for young children entails when they spend time alone with them. Yet when they take paternity leave, the mother is often at home, too.

He also believes that the mother's extended leave tends to reinforce the domestic labour imbalance already in place before the arrival of children. I'll add that a long maternity leave feeds into the workplace discrimination they already face:

People think it's normal for women to take parental leave because they think women know how to raise children. And it always comes back to the breastfeeding argument. But in Quebec, women breastfeed for six months on average. That still leaves another six months. So theoretically, parents could split the leave 50-50. That's not even what the Conseil is recommending, but the breastfeeding argument shouldn't give license to sit back and do nothing. The idea is to leave it up to the parents, but again it needs to be a true choice and not always the mother who automatically takes the leave.[20]

What does he recommend doing to encourage a more equal division of parental leave?

People know the QPIP[21] exists, just like they know employment insurance exists, but they don't always know exactly how it works until they need it. It's the same thing with parental leave. Fathers and mothers find out very little beyond how it functions on a basic level, the "who takes care of my application and when do I apply." They won't check the particulars, rarely look into the process, and often leave it to one of the parents, obviously the mother, to choose the plan. Mothers think the leave automatically falls to them, so sharing it doesn't even cross their minds.[22]

I bring up the possibility of a public campaign via social networks, newspapers, radio, and TV to advertise that the leave can be shared between parents. He likes the idea but doesn't seem to think it's possible given the government's current budget.

RECONFIGURING THE EXISTING MODEL

Christine Fréchette is advocating for an overhaul of the current QPIP. She proposes abolishing parental leave and officially redistributing the weeks between the parents, by granting ten or twelve weeks' paternity leave and the rest to the mother, for example. Any weeks not used by the father would be lost.

The system improves when we impose restrictions. At some point the mother will say to her partner, "Look, I think you can handle it. I've recovered from the birth, I feel like going back to work." Of course we can't assume that's exactly the way things will go, but I think on the whole, more men would step up to their roles and responsibilities if they were home alone with a child rather than be there with the mother.[23]

She acknowledges that change won't happen overnight, but ideally, and in the long run, she argues that men would be more likely to take leave if they were offered a better indexation of benefits. "The CSST [now the CNESST] compensates at 90 percent of wages. Why couldn't the QPIP do the same?" she wonders. "What message are we sending? That we pay less because we think it's a program for women?"

It's incredibly problematic when you stop to think. Although the program was designed to benefit both genders, it is still mainly women who are taking the leave. It's impossible not to see it as a redirection of the overarching sexism— the root of why female-dominated professions remain less well paid.

Fréchette maintains that an improved indexation of QPIP benefits needs to include a cap. "The government needs to know how much it will cost. We need a cap that is fair and representative, indexed from year to year."

THINK BIG!

Marianne Prairie gave birth in 2010 and 2012, and both times she and her partner split the parental leave equally, each receiving half of the benefits. But since they are both self-employed and work from home, they were at home together during the first few days, weeks, and months of their children's lives; the father was never the sole caregiver for any extended period:

> I had "baby-free Fridays" when my boyfriend would take over. It gave me some space, some time out of the house. But he spent less time alone with our daughters, unlike Odile [Archambault of the the blog/book *Maman a un plan*, 'Mother has a plan'] whose spouse took most of the parental leave when she went back to work.[24]

Prairie considers the CSF recommendation of an extended period of father-only leave an excellent idea, but it can be difficult to execute for self-employed mothers who work from home. Not all of these women can afford office space in a shared workplace.

Yet she does believe it is important to divide parental leave between parents.

Giving up part of the parental leave means the mother loses some of her privileges, but it has a lasting impact on the children's education, the family, the relationship, and the division of labour. Of course, not all mothers are eager to get back to work.[25]

I mention what pediatrician Jean-François Chicoine and journalist Nathalie Collard propose in their book:[26] to extend parental leave by six months but keep this period reserved for the father.

It would really help families, affording them greater flexibility and giving value to the father's role. We often hear mothers saying that they don't want to rush back to work, but neither do fathers! They are torn, too. Mothers feel the weight of guilt, the burden of being the primary caretaker. But fathers also bear the burden of tradition in the role of provider. Both suffer from gender stereotypes. I think it's important to support fathers in their role as caregiver.[27]

I couldn't agree more! Why not support mothers in the role of breadwinner? One can dream . . .

The more I write, the more I see an improvement to the Quebec's existing program as critical. Olivier Lamalice would agree. "In Sweden, increasing the length of paternity leave played a large part in improving parental imbalances," he states. But even with two months of paternity leave, Swedish men are no more likely to share the transferrable leave. They take the leave reserved for them, not more.

Our recommendation was supposed to open up a debate, and I think we accomplished our goal with the means we had. Although it isn't perfect, the Swedish system is superior to our current QPIP. The Cadillac would be to have a system like Sweden's, but the CSF cannot make this kind of proposal. It just isn't realistic.[28]

Lamalice tells me that it has always been a struggle when it comes to parental leave, and that each victory has led to small gains. "The Conseil's first recommendation came out in 1978 or 1979 and called for four days' paternity leave. That gives you some idea!"

I believe that audacity and pragmatism can be combined with a real political will. Model programs such as Quebec's daycare system (the CPEs) have gained the admiration and envy of the rest of Canada, and even made waves south of the border. Before the QPIP came into effect in 2006, paternity leave was five days—just one day longer than the Conseil had pushed for more than thirty-five years ago. The bar was raised practically overnight, when leave increased from five days to five weeks. It pays to think big! And since breastfeeding is the primary argument parents use to justify a mother-only model or a superficial division of leave,[29] it seems necessary to increase paternity leave without cutting into weeks intended for the mother.

Jean-Philippe Pleau couldn't agree more:

As it stands today, parental leave just reproduces the system of the past. I have friends in their mid-thirties who had children very young, back when paternity leave was only five days. It's astounding when you think about it—it wasn't even that long ago! Up until 2006, we were churning out potentially absent fathers. Now paternity leave is three to five weeks, but in those first weeks you don't really have time to enjoy it. You're dealing with the baby's constant feeding schedule and you're tired. The QPIP was lauded as an incredible advance [because, I'd like to point out, we had SO far to go], but three to five weeks is a joke. Then we say fathers aren't involved enough .... I get it, but we aren't really encouraging anything different from a systemic perspective.[30]

For Pleau, taking a share of the parental leave feels a bit like stealing from the mother:

You feel bad. If paternity leave were longer, I think then we'd be talking. My daughters saw me go right back to work after my youngest was born. I had to explain that it wasn't because I didn't want to stay home. Since that's how the system is made, I have to address the representations it projects onto my daughters, to make sure they understand this is just the way things are, whether I like it or not. I can see how men might get upset by the idea of a longer paternity leave, as if someone were attacking their masculinity. But I hope that by the time my son is old enough to be having kids, he'll be allowed a paternity leave worthy of its name.[31]

Laurent Turcot also believes we should extend paternity leave without cutting into parental leave. He is a special case; he was able to carve out his own extended leave by taking a semester off from the university. For him, sharing the thirty-two week parental leave was out of the question. "I couldn't take [those weeks] away from Stéphanie. She needed them. She breastfed our children for thirteen and seventeen months." He doesn't support the CSF's proposal, because he sees it as taking away from the mother in order to give to the father.

But he maintains that the five weeks currently reserved for fathers should be taken immediately after the child is born.

> Especially when your wife's had a C-section—she needs you. Either take paternity leave right away, or don't take it at all. And if you take it, you've got eight weeks. That would be a good policy. The mother needs the full parental leave; she's tired, especially if she's breastfeeding.[32]

Rachel Chagnon is also in favour of extending father-only leave without reducing either the maternity or parental leaves in place:

> One of the frustrating results of the current system is that what it gives to one parent, it takes from the other. Not all women want to give up their parental leave. It's almost like taking a year sabbatical; mom can be at home caring for her children, watching them grow, without having to think about work.

> Even if you love your job, I've rarely seen a woman devastated because she didn't go back to work after six months.[33]

But I've known women who were tired of staring at their baby all day, who missed adult conversation and felt intellectually under-stimulated. These women oppose the sacrosanct dictum that motherhood be enjoyable and wholly fulfilling. Yet mothers who long to return to work during their parental leave feel inept, guilt-ridden, judged, ashamed, and selfish, so they just grin and bear it.

LEVELLING DOWN?

Let's revisit the idea of extending the leave reserved for fathers, a proposal I wholeheartedly support. To avoid gender-biased treatment in the workforce, fathers must be given an equal amount of leave following the birth of a child and take time off work just as often as mothers do when the child is sick.

An improved parental leave policy will not spirit away the persistent double standard in our patriarchal society that dictates notions of fatherhood vastly differ from those of motherhood.

Rachel Chagnon cites the classic example of a mother who needs to take her child to a dentist appointment. When she shows up late to work afterwards, she blames it on a flat tire; an accident will seem more acceptable than the truth regarding her parental responsibilities—an explanation sure to make colleagues, women and men alike, sigh with exasperation.

The opposite is true for fathers. If Dad gets a flat tire, he'll say he had to take his kid to the dentist since he knows his colleagues—the women at least—will find it admirable. (Remember Laurent Turcot's anecdote about the trip to the doctor.)

Given the above, Chagnon wonders if a father's absence during parental leave will be read in the same way. "Are we going to keep building fathers up to be models of self-sacrifice the second they get involved, but still consider mothers to be problematic?" she asks.

She touches on something I addressed in the third chapter: bosses will react in many ways, but they certainly won't swoon before a male employee who brings his child to doctor's appointments or takes some of the parental leave.

When we consider professions that lose their prestige as they become feminized, or men who are affected by the pressure of unrealistic beauty standards projected by the media, will improving mothers' lots and redistributing parental responsibility harm men? Will it divide male employees into two categories: the top-notch childfree worker and the problematic parent? In other words, does the quest for equality tend to drag us down? Is the glass half empty or half full?

The indomitable optimist in me believes that it's worth the fight; action is always better than inaction. Extending paternity leave would send the right signal to normalize parenthood in the workplace, confirming that work-family alignment isn't a uniquely feminine responsibility.

The vast majority of people have children, after all; it's ridiculous to ignore this fact in the professional sphere, to think that the workplace should consider it a non-issue, as if people floated around in their own little bubbles, as if work had no effect on family life and vice versa. . . . Quick, hide that family!

A PLEA FOR GREATER FLEXIBILITY

In addition to extending paternity leave, the QPIP system needs to be more flexible; both parents and employers would benefit. The idea would be to increase the length of parental leave by allowing the employee a gradual, part-time return to work. This would create a smoother back-to-work transition and result in less stress for the whole family—especially for mothers, since in the majority of cases they take more of the parental leave and are considered the primary parent. The employer would benefit from a more relaxed employee, one who is less likely to face physical or mental health problems related to the stress of balancing a career and a family. These include hypertension, insomnia, burnout, depression, alcoholism, and the list goes on.

Olivier Lamalice reminds me that not all sectors provide access to parental leave. He

highlights single mothers, those working min-
imum-wage jobs, and those whose work split
shifts.

> The QPIP was designed for middle-class couples
> who work Monday to Friday, nine to five. Offering
> benefits at 70 percent to a single mother is com-
> pletely unrealistic. She won't make ends meet.
> That's where the struggle is. At the same time, we
> can't criticize [the QPIP] too much, because it's still
> a good program. But that shouldn't stop us from
> questioning it and looking for ways to improve it.[34]

And he's right. It's time to think about what
those changes would look like. Wouldn't human
decency suggest payouts at 100 percent, rather
than 70 percent, for a woman earning minimum
wage? Lamalice agrees.

> We could say that below a certain income thresh-
> old the benefits would be at 100 percent. Otherwise
> it creates a spiral of poverty and social assistance
> that can be difficult to break. We need to do more
> research on disadvantaged women in Quebec—
> who head three quarters of single-parent house-
> holds—and adapt family policies accordingly.
> These women are struggling, and right now par-
> ental leave is not adapted to the realities of parents
> with unconventional schedules and single-par-
> ent families. They can't stand alone; these things
> are interrelated. So the most important thing
> is to make the QPIP more flexible, even before
> extending paternity benefits. Everyone should be
> able to benefit. We should report leave by the day,

not by the week, extend the window of opportunity, and allow for part-time leave benefits. This would offer significant support to self-employed women[35] and encourage a return to the workforce. Because we know it's almost always women who stay home when a child is sick. It's all connected."[36]

Amen.

ARE GENERATION Y/MILLENIAL PARENTS MORE EQUAL?

It's winter 2016, and I open the most recent edition of *Trente,* the publication of Quebec's federation of professional journalists (FPJQ). In it, an article about "life after journalism" profiles a former female Radio-Canada journalist who decided to change directions and go into public relations. She talks about how difficult it is to come to terms with giving up a career she was so passionate about. So why the career shift? She wanted a more stable schedule in order to start a family.

I wonder if a man would have made the same decision. I highly doubt it. We aren't as far as we think from the time when women left the workforce once they got married or pregnant. Today women aren't making the same kinds of sacrifices, but they're making them just the same.

The heterosexual couple is still a structure that favours men, argues Rachel Chagnon.

> For women, being part of a couple is more of a challenge, something that requires work. For men, it's more about their personal well-being. In other words, the person who gets the most out of a relationship, who gets the biggest return on investment, is still the man. Things haven't changed all that much.[1]

When it comes down to it, is the couple—and by extension, the family—subjugating women? By that, I mean the frequently advantageous economic situation a relationship offers, since it is an unfortunate reality that men still out-earn women in nearly all industries and across nearly all age groups in Canada and Quebec.[2] But financial dependence can have disastrous consequences, such as forcing women to stay in toxic and violent relationships.

Isn't the couple a subjugating force since it also represents a necessary step for most women who hope to become mothers? Girls are taught very early on that the ultimate life goal, the main proof of success, is becoming a mother. In these conditions, the fear of missing out becomes a powerful driving force.

Could it be that this time-sensitive, and thus frantic, search for a mate is at the root of an inequity for women? That, despite themselves, women end up far too often trapped in inadequate relationships, tolerating the unacceptable? Could the "equation" be that they have internalized the toxic logic whereby finding the father of their children is a stroke of luck, PLUS this man is doing them some sort of favour, which EQUALS: it is up to them to make the most significant personal and professional sacrifices for the good of the family?

It was hard to write that sentence. I feel my stomach sink, not unlike the ominous sensation I get when I'm about to receive bad news. Some truths I would rather ignore. I can't be the only one choking over that idea—I bet many readers are, too. The "likeable" feminists have always been those who don't shock, who don't make us feel guilty. Yet I feel guilty for writing these cold hard truths.

But I feel the need to shake things up. After all, suffragettes didn't get the right to vote by drinking tea in their sitting rooms. And as a wise colleague once told me while I was serving on the Association féminine d'éducation et d'action sociale (AFEAS), a moderate feminist organization if there ever was one, we owe advances in family law and access to abortion to the radical feminists of the 1970s. So I maintain that some things need to be said, even—and especially—the inconvenient truths.

No, relationships aren't the stuff of fairy tales. Yes, there is an economic affiliation in play, particularly given that wage losses, instability, part-time work, and invisible and unpaid labour (caregivers, stay-at-home mothers, etc.) more often affect women. None of that has changed, even if it is 2018.

I'm tempted to ask the reverse: why we would expect things to have changed in such a short amount of time? Essentialist, gendered, stereotyped, and sexist attitudes are still deeply entrenched. We cannot expect a complete restructuring when it comes to relationships and parenthood in the scarcely fifty years since women flooded the workforce (just the blink of an eye in the history of humanity!). It's what annoys me the most when people claim we've already achieved equality, that "it's all settled, so quit whining." I find this unbelievably naïve; it shows a blatant lack of sociological and historical perspective.

I think the next time I come across one of these Pollyannas, I'll ask whether they really got the six pack from that Ab Roller or the hot summer body from that cling film body wrap...

DOING AWAY WITH THE IMAGE OF THE CONTROLLING WIFE

You can tell that Marianne Prairie has given a lot of thought to issues of parenthood. Her comments are honest, fair, and insightful. She argues that there is a fine line between the glorified, unattainable image of a mother, as discussed in the second chapter, and the archetypal domineering woman who wears the proverbial pants. It's quite the catch-22 when you think about it: so much pressure to become the perfect mother, only to end up reproached for being controlling—it's a paradox, a double bind.

Prairie and I talk about what I see as the icing on the cake: how spouses guilt-trip mothers for doing too much, criticizing them for not delegating enough household chores (as if they're champing at the bit!). She agrees, and gives me another perspective:

> It's complicated, because controlling women really do exist. I'm trying to work on it myself. But why are we like this? How do some guys just kick back and fail to see what needs to be done, and then need reminding? Well it's probably because when we're entertaining and the house isn't perfectly clean or things aren't done well enough, it's the mother who gets judged.

BOOM. It's much easier to be relaxed when it isn't your dignity that's on the line.

Some would argue that women should just care less. True, part of the solution lies in women letting go. But again, that's easier said than done. And again, it's always the women putting in the effort.

Telling women to care less is easy if you aren't the one being judged. It's akin to saying: "You'll be judged and I won't, but I'm sorry if that bothers you." Once again, we're seeing gender inequality at work.

And for every gift a child fails to give a teacher, every birthday party they attend empty-handed, the mothers are the ones who will suffer. And this is exactly what mothers try to avoid. They care about the consequences giving up the control will have on their children. So they continue to perform what we call *emotional labour*.

HAVE ROLES REALLY CHANGED?

Marianne Prairie talks about how tempting it can be for couples to simply reproduce models they have grown up with.

> I can totally understand how some families adopt stereotypical roles right off the bat, because it's a lot of work to rethink and question everything, to redefine yourself. Like my boyfriend said recently, working as a team—truly working together—is hard. Just imagine when the project is a little human being! Couples often work in silos, each in their own little corner. Many aren't equipped enough. We're in the process of redefining roles, but it takes a lot of communication. That's the biggest hurdle.

She reminds me that members of Generation Y like herself, the ones who are outspoken on issues of equality, self-respect, and a healthy work-life balance, are just now becoming parents:

> Guys who have grown up in feminist house-holds will frequently notice what needs to be done around the house and will take on family

responsibilities, since they were raised to do their share of the chores. A boy raised by a single mother will be more aware of what it takes to keep the boat afloat. These men are more sensitive and more aware, unlike children who were raised in a more traditional household.

Does she believe it's inevitable for most women to end up bearing the weight of worry and family responsibilities?

Right now we're seeing a shift in parenting roles. People are questioning the division of labour, family organization, and worry sharing. I've been a mother for seven years. Our generation of parents can see that there's a problem. We're in the process of evolving, of experimenting. Talking about the growing popularity of policies that promote work-family balance like working from home or a father taking paternity leave—whether he has to justify himself or not—, these are all recent social phenomena in the past five to ten years. We're thinking about these questions, we're defining another aspect of parenthood. It isn't easy, so we're bound to run into issues.

Jean-Philippe Pleau is fairly optimistic view about the future.

I think attitudes are changing. I see it when I look at my friends, but also when I go to Quebec City to visit family. These ideas [of parental equality] resonate with a lot of people. But I don't think we've adapted our services, programs, and attitudes yet.

Laurent Turcot, whom I would argue is best equipped from a historical perspective in light of his job, is more pessimistic:

> Humans only reproduce what they know. Equality is fundamentally impossible in our society, which categorizes people according to their social utility. Historically, a woman's utility was to procreate and care for the children. It's always been like that, just like how society determined a woman was worth less than a man. Why would that change now?

I suspect he's trying to provoke me, in the good sense of the word, in the same way he must rattle his students from time to time. There is no doubt we are averse to change, but I think gender stereotypes can stifle men, too. They have a stake in seeing a change. Like Marianne Prairie argues, they feel stifled by the traditional role of provider and sincerely want to spend more time with their children. I think about Jean-Philippe Pleau, who felt torn to return to work after his paternity leave was up, who hopes his son won't have to experience the same thing.

I wasn't wrong: Laurent Turcot was only half-serious. "When a historian tells you it's been this way since the dawn of mankind and that nothing's going to change, he's a bad historian," he remarks. Then again, he's no stranger to the magnitude and scope of the stereotypes and social constructs we have to demolish. Another

major obstacle to achieving gender equality is
something he calls the death of social empathy:

> Four hundred years ago, social empathy was gov-
> erned by religion, both Christianity and Islam,
> which dictated that we had to help the less fortun-
> ate. In the 17th century we see poverty becoming
> criminalized, the idea that it's your own fault if
> you are poor, that you're a vector of social dis-
> order. At the same time there was a rise in the
> functionalization of bodies: people had to make
> themselves useful. Under Louis XIV in France and
> George III in England, people were forced to work
> for the state. Without social empathy, exploita-
> tion becomes normalized. You are subjugated, you
> must remain subjugated. You are a woman, you
> must remain subjugated. I need not have empathy
> for you, because society has assigned you a role
> you must fill.

There is a parallel to be made with our own
society, where individualism has taken on reli-
gious status. Our tendency to relegate social
issues to the personal sphere, to people's private
lives, keeps structural problems in place world-
wide. An insidious individualism often hides
behind what some would call "common sense." It
is this lack of social empathy that prevents many
men (and women!) from feeling the least bit concerned by feminist issues, as if equal opportunity
only applies to women and can be overcome if
they try hard enough. So let's go girl, you can do
it! As Turcot explains:

If we look back two centuries ago, we think people were backward. But just imagine how people in the year 2217 will look at Quebec in the 21st century. It's incredibly difficult to fight sexism on a daily basis. We've got to prepare our children, tell my daughter that when a kid at her daycare says superheroes are only for guys she's allowed to kick his ass.

Can we collectively redefine ourselves? Perhaps, but it will take a great deal of effort and political will. And it won't happen in one single generation. I know we put all our faith in millennials, but expecting major change from them is like hoping to achieve equality overnight. And that's voluntarism.

In the meantime, how can we ensure that Quebec becomes a society in which, at the very least, we eliminate the reflex to dismiss an applicant of child-bearing age?

How can we ensure that young candidates, regardless of gender, are hired with full knowledge that they will likely take an extended parental leave—and that such circumstances are considered a reality of workplace management and not an exceptional and irritating complication?

I'll detail my game plan in the conclusion.

NECESSARY CHANGES

When I think about motherhood in 2018, it seems to go hand in hand with professional burnout. Often the most productive employees are the ones who eventually fall in battle, the ones always asked to do more while constantly depleting their financial, emotional, and material resources. At the end of the day, bosses are pushing these model employees to the end of their rope.

It seems all working mothers suffer the same injustices. They've seen their free time melt away like snow in the sun for the past thirty years, yet now more than ever they are bombarded with dictums on being the perfect mother: "Nurse as long as you can," "Cook healthy meals for the family," "Don't send your children to daycare or summer camp," "Lose that pregnancy weight as soon as you can." All these instructions, all this unsolicited and unwelcome advice only adds to the pressure.

Working mothers are overwhelmed by guilt. They are stressed and exhausted. Though fathers are more involved in family life than ever before, women still carry the burden of running a happy, balanced household. They are deemed the "competent" and "responsible" parent by default. Everything they do is considered normal and expected, including the majority of household chores.[1]

I had a revelation in the fall of 2015 when *Planète F* had me cover a talk on this issue,[2] co-presented by the YMCAs of Québec, the Conseil des Montréalaises, and the Institut du Nouveau Monde. At one point during her speech, Ariane Émond, who co-founded the magazine *La vie en rose* in the late 1970s (to which my own blog, *La semaine rose*, is a rather thinly veiled tribute), remarked, "If someone had told me it would take forty years for men to do ten hours of housework a week, I'd have fainted." The pioneer of feminism in Quebec assumed the private struggle over household equality would be brief. Things were changing, after all. Equality had to be right around the corner! How disappointing . . .

We have made slow but undeniable progress when it comes to equality in the home. And I think the population still has a slight lead over political decision-makers. As proof, voters show no gender bias, though parties remain reluctant to actively court female candidates even while spurred on to meet gender quotas.

But beyond just resistance to change, we still come up against powerful and persistent stereotypes related to parenthood. Contrary to popular belief, we have a long way to go before we see a shift in attitudes. It's disturbing to think that less than a hundred years ago, most Quebecers were in favour of denying women the right to vote, that the first women was elected to the National Assembly[3] just over fifty years ago. Our descendants will smile sanctimoniously when they learn that as recently as the early 21st century, people still held the antiquated belief that women are biologically programmed to be natural caregivers and family organizers.

With every passing generation, people think they have attained peak modernity; they bask in the glory of having reached the pinnacle of civilization. This was the case in Western Europe in the 19th century, just as it was for the ancient Greeks. It's this same reflex that today prompts many men—and women—to believe that we have achieved gender equality. Feminism is a thing of the past! But as long as parenthood is considered primarily a woman's domain, these changes remain a fantasy.

A COMPLEX REALITY

A political system that lacks parity notwithstanding, I have attempted to demonstrate what equality would look like in this book. I interviewed an equal number of women and men to broaden the perspectives presented. I think it's safe to say it has been a truly gender-balanced conversation about parenting issues.

I haven't overlooked the fact that this book focuses on heterosexual families, though we could learn a thing or two from single-sex parents (I mentioned this in Chapter 2). This is a compelling field of research I hope to explore one day.

Nor does this book fully chart the complex realities single parents face, compounded when one of the parents is totally absent. This is a reality for many mothers.[4] Some of my close friends have separated from their child's father, and letting go of the idea of a traditional family has been a painful process. A few of these women have a new partner, others are unattached. But I also know extremely courageous women who chose to be single parents right from the start. One benefited from a large network of support, reinforcing the notion that it takes a village to raise a child; the other found herself more isolated and she struggled.

In both cases, these women are proud of what they have achieved. But let's not forget that they chose to take full responsibility for raising a child alone. It is common to feel frustrated and angry in the face of injustice and a lack of control. For these friends who never conceived childbirth as a team project, the disappointment of a labour imbalance and an under-involved spouse were not part of the equation—though this doesn't mean their lives are picture perfect.

I want to make it clear that I'm not judging women who decide to leave or reduce their participation in the workforce to devote more time to their family. But I do want to guarantee that these so-called personal choices are, in fact, choices. Given the current state of things, I'm not sure it's ever a choice. If we keep giving dolls to just our girls, if we keep signing up our daughters but not our sons for babysitting courses, if our reflex is still to fawn over girls and come down hard on the boys, we cannot claim women are making neutral choices in a neutral parenting environment. And I'll go one step further: I don't think men have the luxury of true choice, either.

Caring for children is so gender-segregated that it is almost always the mothers who volunteer in schools and daycares and on school boards, while men chair or sit on steering committees—seen as a more prestigious activity that directly influences the capitalist system in which we live. Of course, women's invisible and voluntary labour changes the world too, especially when these women work with future generations. And caring for others is invaluable and admirable work (though the virtue accorded these so-called "feminine" jobs can come back to bite them; it's a very fine line between being selfless and being exploited). Yet women's unpaid work is belittled and ill recognized, even taken for granted, as if it were the natural course of things (our old friend essentialism!). We need to realign ourselves and integrate our practices with what we preach.

ENDURING CONCERNS

I'd like to give this book a happy ending, an open-ended conclusion full of hope. But I can't write something I don't believe to be true. I'm generally an optimist, but admittedly not about what lies ahead. The only way we can preserve past gains and take steps to achieve equal opportunity for women is to remain collectively vigilant. But right now, I don't see that happening. The notion that we've achieved equality is so widespread that it risks undermining all that's been achieved for women, many of whom have internalized inequalities to the point that they no longer even perceive them. I hear all too often that dads are "watching" their kids. No, a father doesn't watch his kids; he takes care of them and raises them.

If we want to stem inequalities, we must start by identifying the problems and staying alert. Together, we can push for change. For employers, this means continuing to self-monitor, to avoid making sexist decisions like turning down women of child-bearing age or more mature candidates who are often at the height of experience and availability after having devoted years to raising a family. Women are often targets of ageism.

Maintaining non-sexist hiring practices requires vigilance, introspection, and humility.

We have to be careful about the words we use. Terms like parental "leave" or work-family "balance" are problematic. The first minimizes the burden of parental responsibility during those first months of a child's life while the second stigmatizes family life (with a tacit nod to women) by rendering the family a burden on the career.

We need to take a collective interest in the well-being of parents across Quebec. I see a frustrating tendency towards a subtle "live and let live" attitude, regardless of the topic of debate, that stops discussion in its tracks. In a society at the height of individualism, it is easy to reduce everything to personal choice without even considering the context. Yet choices are not made in a vacuum, and individuals are not impermeable to outside pressure of all sources. We live in a society where tradition weighs heavy, where women are still relegated to the background.

What can we do right now to encourage parental equality? We could start with the following. First, it is high time that fathers-to-be flipped through a few parenting books so that women aren't the only ones consulting the myriad publications being endlessly rolled out.[5] I also believe it's just as important for fathers to belong to local parent resource groups on Facebook and other platforms in addition to subscribing to parenting magazines.

In short, I want to tell the guys: stop leaving things up to women, stop relying on them to the point they end up with all the family responsibilities on their shoulders!

And it begins with your sons. Sign them up for babysitting classes: it's a good way to earn pocket money, an honourable and educative experience as much for boys as for girls. And while we're at it, give your little boys dolls to play with (we need to find another name—"dolls" is so loaded). Let them nurture and cuddle their babies so it becomes normal for them to take care of children from an early age.

A COMMENDABLE INITIATIVE

As I write these words, a blazing sun shines over Quebec and the UN has just appointed American actress Anne Hathaway to be its Goodwill Ambassador. Her mission will be to highlight challenges faced by working mothers. As if the universe is responding to my anger this past winter, this announcement is encouraging . . . to some extent.

In the Agence France-Presse release announcing collaboration with the actress, Director of UN Women Phumzile Mlambo-Ngcuka addressed the "motherhood penalty" which rang out like music to my ears:

The "motherhood penalty"—which means that when they become mothers, women's pay and opportunities at work suffer—is a particularly insidious demonstration of gender inequality in the workplace. For too long it has been difficult or impossible to view raising a child as being truly an equal responsibility for both parents.[6]

When I think of the media coverage previous UN Women ambassador, British actress Emma Watson, set off with her "HeForShe" campaign, I think we have something to celebrate. The initiative turned many men into objective feminist allies and popularized the movement with young girls. It is my hope that ideas put forth in this book will also be the focus of mass media campaigns.

Yet I fear this new campaign by UN Women will have less impact. The media craze is selective; it thrives on the exceptional and the surprising, on news that makes a big splash.

This was the case with Emma Watson: her status as "prodigy," which she owes to her youth (she was twenty-four at the time of her UN speech) as well as her role of brainiac in the *Harry Potter* movies, piqued the curiosity of newsrooms around the world. In contrast, what could be less exciting than hearing from a thirty-three-year-old new mother, an actress who supports equal opportunity for working mothers? Boring! It's a newsflash that belongs in the lifestyle section, today's "women's pages" of the past. New look, same content. I really hope I'm wrong on this one.

POLITICAL WILL IS KEY

The issue of equal parenting is so vast, it's difficult to do it justice in such a short book. Time and again, I felt as though each door I opened led to ten others. But it's vital to bring the crux of the matter to the forefront of public awareness.

Men still hold the power in Quebec (and elsewhere), both in terms of influence and positions held, as well as managing budgets.[7] I smile when I hear people say that if men could get pregnant, there'd be more access to abortion in the United States. And around the world, I'd argue, especially in rural areas where there is reduced access to services. By this logic, we can ask ourselves: once men start having to balance a family and a career to the extent women do, will we begin to see improvements in government policy and more flexibility on the part of employers? I'll let you guess my answer . . . YES!

So instead of reducing Quebec Parental Insurance Program contributions, why not improve the design and benefits? It's a gem of a program that doesn't cost much collectively. It affords our society great possibility for advancement as we work towards equal opportunity for women. We should be proud of it; we should promote it.

And don't tell me that this is impossible, that it's too costly, that the state's pockets are empty. Because that would indicate that as a society we cannot afford gender equality. Managing the treasury is a matter of choice, of priorities, of orientation, and political will. We've got no problem paying 30 percent extra to corrupt contractors for a tiny stretch of highway or a new bridge or overpass, and it's OK to look the other way on tax evasion when there are plenty of solutions out there—*these* we can afford? Ensuring gender equality isn't a luxury; it's a necessity. Not striving in its direction is to govern with a sexist hand.

I've come up with a four-pronged approach to fixing things. First, we need to adapt the Quebec Parental Insurance Program to the realities of single parents and parents with nonstandard schedules by allowing them to take part-time leave over a longer period of time. To do this would mean retooling the weekly benefits calculator, based on the old employment insurance model, in favour of a daily calculator. Doing so would also benefit self-employed women like hairstylists and aestheticians. A more flexible QPIP would help women maintain and return to their jobs.

Next, to ensure access to parental leave for vulnerable employees, particularly in the service industry, we'll need to bolster the health, safety and employment equity board, Quebec's CNESST. The organization must take real action against delinquent employers, who punish employees who take parental leave by doing away with their priority and modifying or reducing their hours. This involves sending inspectors into the field, imposing high fines, and creating a system for filing anonymous complaints on behalf of frequently mistreated labourers working in non-unionized environments, where personnel management is often arbitrary. These employees may justly fear reprisal when they call attention to the abuse.

Another parental insurance program improvement involves significantly increasing benefits to salaried workers living below the poverty line— maternity, paternity, and parental leaves combined. The lowest earners in society should not have to take a further financial hit to take care of their children. In reality, such leaves prove inaccessible to low income earners. But everyone, without exception, should have the opportunity to stop working to care for their child during the first months of life. This is about equal rights for women, since it is still the vast majority of mothers who take parental leave.

Finally, we need to extend leave reserved for fathers. Like Laurent Turcot, Rachel Chagnon, and Jean-Philippe Pleau, I do not believe we should take from the mothers to give to the fathers. We must invest further. Because true reconciliation of work and family responsibilities often begins once the long parental leave ends— once the mother all too commonly becomes the primary parent, the "control tower," leaving the father to settle into the role of support staff. This leads to an imbalance in domestic and familial responsibilities. And unfortunately, too many overworked, exhausted mothers of young children voluntarily reduce their hours or leave their jobs altogether, either temporarily or permanently. These represent total losses in tax revenue for the province.

The Quebec Parental Insurance Program is financed through workers' income. Investing in a longer paternity leave will result in a more balanced division of parental responsibilities, leading to a higher rate of employment for women that will benefit society as a whole (and promote gender equality—everybody wins!).

The improved plan[8] should offer paternity[9] and maternity leaves of equal length and retain the weeks of transferrable parental leave. And the QPIP 2.0 should give fathers strong incentive to take part of their leave without the mother present.

A father should be able to divide his eighteen-week paternity leave in order to stay home with the mother for ten to fourteen weeks after the child is born, for instance, reserving the rest for the end of the parental leave once the mother has returned to work.

A father who stays home alone with his child hones his parenting skills; he becomes a more self-confident dad. This is the best way to achieve true co-parenting. The current system locks spouses into traditional roles. Extending paternity leave and encouraging fathers to spend some of this time solo parenting is an absolute must if we want to guarantee greater gender equality for future generations.

To echo Christine Fréchette, equality is not a zero sum game; everyone can win. A long paternity leave would activate childcare responses long associated with women and enrich a father's relationship with his children. Doing so would also dispel the notion of "mother knows best."

Giving a longer leave to fathers would be the death knell of employers' all-too-common reflex to eye female applicants suspiciously, since male applicants would become just as likely to take off for a long period. And since parenthood would be seen as a shared responsibility, it would pose less of a hurdle to women's career advancement. We would see less of the types of discrimination mentioned in Chapter 1.

Establishing a longer, non-transferrable paternity leave would result in a major shift in attitudes, both in the personal and professional spheres. It would also be instrumental in curbing employers' perceptions that starting a family is a uniquely female issue. A family would become a fact of life, or one that affects both genders equally, at the very least.

A LEAP FORWARD

The role of political leaders has always been to guide the population towards the common good.

Not everyone governs with this goal in mind, but such is their role—even their duty. Quebec's Quiet Revolution of the 1960s was a major leap forward. Nearly six decades later, the time has come for Quebec to up the ante.

Now, in 2018, we must return to our progressive values by collectively laying the foundation for future generations, just as those before us have done. Women fought for equality, as was their right. Today, no one questions their struggles. But we aren't there yet; we still have a long way to go.

It is time we bring parenthood out of the private sphere. Like any other social issue, individual goodwill won't suffice. An unequal division of parenting responsibilities and professional limitations imposed on women are systemic problems; Quebec must enact measures to counter them. It falls to us to ensure that when the government manifests support for gender equality, they follow up with concrete actions. We cannot expect broad social change to appear overnight if it remains on a personal voluntary basis, in the comfort of our own homes. Especially when it comes to parenthood, an issue rife with stereotypes that conjures up endless clichés and images we're bombarded with in our day to day.

Without responsible leadership and a strong political will, we simply won't succeed; we'll be kept swimming in circles for decades. The signal must come from above. The signal must be clear.

While the recommendation of the Quebec status of women board, the CSF, to reserve three weeks' parental leave for the sole use of fathers may not be perfect, it highlights the long road ahead before parenting responsibilities are shared equally between fathers and mothers.

Egalitarian parenting is one of the struggles—if not the main one—facing women who hope to one day achieve equal opportunity. And there's still a lot to do. For instance, we must revisit Quebec's family law in order to protect mothers in common-law relationships, as discussed in Chapter 2. But first, we have to strike at the root of the issue: we must change attitudes about parenthood, starting the moment women see that faint blue line.

Access to a long paternity leave and even cases where fathers take a portion—in some cases, half—of the parental leave would solidify the bonds between a father and his child. It would also take us one step closer to domestic and parental parity. Most importantly, it would put an end to insidious, systemic, discrimination in the workplace against women.

In short, such a measure may well lead to a revolution of equality in the labour market. It is the duty of our political leaders to take us in bold, new directions by enacting the necessary reforms.

The takeaway is crystal clear: the fact parental leave is taken overwhelmingly by women hurts their hiring prospects, impedes career progress, and produces a gender income gap with long-lasting impacts. We must acknowledge this reality. The idea is not to attach too much importance to a career; rather, we should strive to align all spheres of our life, for every citizen, regardless of gender.

A woman should not be reduced to a single dimension once she becomes a mother. That greater parenting responsibilities fall to mothers is a social construct we must dismantle. The government must do its fair share to ensure that one day this historic imbalance preventing women from thriving is eliminated. The time has come. And it includes both an overhaul to the QPIP by extending paternity benefits and a public campaign to encourage fathers to stay home with their children for a longer period of time.

Christine Fréchette, who has dedicated much of her time to developing a Quebec Parental Insurance Program worthy of its name, believes that it is time for a reform. So do I. So here we are. Fréchette reminds me of a quote by Victor Hugo, and I couldn't agree more: "Nothing is more powerful than an idea whose time has come."

Women can "have it all"—a fulfilling career *and* a gratifying family life—the moment men want exactly the same thing. This is my greatest wish. For men to want to "have it all" too.

TABLE I

Current plans

Type of Benefits	Basic plan			Special plan	
	Maximum weeks	Percentage of average weekly income		Maximum weeks	Percentage of average weekly income
Maternity	18	70%		15	75%
Paternity	5	70%		3	75%
Parental (transferrable)	32	7 weeks at 70% 25 weeks at 55%		25	75%

TABLE II

Improved plans

Type of Benefits	Basic plan			Special plan	
	Maximum weeks	Percentage of average weekly income		Maximum weeks	Percentage of average weekly income
Maternity	18	70%		15	75%
Paternity	18	70%		15	75%
Parental (transferrable)	32	7 weeks at 70% 25 weeks at 55%		25	75%

ACKNOWLEDGEMENTS

I would like to thank Marie-Claude Fortin, my wonderful editor at Leméac, without whom none of this would have been possible; my friend Pascale Navarro, who believed in my project and encouraged me from the start; as well as interviewees Marianne Prairie, Olivier Lamalice, Rachel Chagnon, Jean-Philippe Pleau, Christine Fréchette, and Laurent Turcot for all their time, thoughts, and generosity. A big thanks to Julie Miville-Dechêne for letting me pick her brain during our travels throughout Quebec, to Nathalie Collard for helping me change the world over a good glass (or two) of wine, and to Martine Letarte for her enthusiasm and precious leads. I am immensely grateful for my good friend Daphné Angiolini, whose voyage through motherhood was the spark that led me to write the book you are holding. Thanks to all of my mom friends who shared their stories with me; the same goes for my dad friends. Finally, thank you to my part-ner, Philippe Boisvert, for his patience, which was regularly put to the test during the writing of this book; as well as my family (I'm thinking of you, Robert Hamelin, Élaine Simard, Yannick Hamelin, and Marie-Lune Brisebois); and to all my friends (that's you, Jean-Sébastien Burguière!) for their encouragement.

For the English edition, special thanks to Arielle Aaronson for the excellent translation, Bronwyn Averette for proofreading, and Toula Drimonis for writing the Foreword, and to Robin Philpot of Baraka Books for sharing the conviction that this book should be available in North America in the language of Shakespeare.

NOTES

BUILDING ON QUEBEC'S EXPERIENCE IN PARENTAL EQUALITY

1. "Les enfants coûtent plus cher aux meres" by Isabelle Porter, *Le Devoir*, May 9, 2018.

INTRODUCTION. DAYS OF ANGER

1. Nathalie Collard, *Qui s'occupe du souper?* (Montreal: Québec Amérique, 2016), 200.

2. Michelle J. Budig, "The Fatherhood Bonus and The Motherhood Penalty: Parenthood and the Gender Gap in Pay," *Third Way*, September 2, 2014, www.thirdway.org/report/the-fatherhood-bonus-and-the-motherhood-penalty-parent-hood-and-the-gender-gap-in-pay, accessed September 1, 2016.

3. The terms "parental leave"—a period of twenty-five or thirty-two weeks, depending on the type of plan chosen, and "maternity leave," both issued through the Quebec Parental Insurance Plan (QPIP)—are often conflated and lumped together in popular language. While an exclusive maternity leave exists, it consists of fifteen or eighteen weeks while paternity leave lasts either three or five weeks. See Table 1.

4. Amélie Daoust-Boisvert, "Des femmes médecins victimes de discrimination à l'embauche. 30% d'entre elles sont questionnées sur leur intention d'avoir des enfants, selon un sondage," *Le Devoir*, November 25, 2016 www.ledevoir.com/

societe/sante/485629/medecins-des-femmes-victimes-de-discrimination-a-l-embauche, accessed January 9, 2017.

5. Anne Gaignaire, "Entrepreneur et parent: l'art de jongler avec les horaires," *Les affaires*, August 17, 2015, www.lesaffaires.com/dossier/petites-entreprises-grands-defis/entrepreneur-et-parent--lart-de-jongler-avec-les-horaires/580893, accessed September 19, 2016.

6. Sandra Mathieu, "Conciliation grossesse-travail: 'Loin d'une culture d'accommodements,'" *Métro*, October 25, 2015, www.journalmetro.com/plus/carrieres/863369/conciliation-grossesse-travail-loin-dune-culture-daccommodements/, accessed September 19, 2016.

7. Stéphanie Grammond, "La retraite à la sauce libérale," *La Presse*, October 25, 2015, www.plus.lapresse.ca/screens/f039f198-a8db-4110-a3ca-d0f047ee631d%7C_0.html, accessed September 19, 2016.

8. L'effet A is an initiative of Sun Life Financial Quebec executive Isabelle Hudon. It offers a wide range of projects aimed at boosting women's ambition and encourages them to reach the highest levels of decision-making. The movement's mission of empowerment seeks to embolden women. The problem with this approach is that the initiative tends to minimize or altogether mask the systemic obstacles which stand in the way of women's liberation, reducing the idea of "success" in terms of career ambitions and aspirations to a simple question of personal preference. In contrast, the book in your hands seeks to demonstrate that despite everyone's good will, as long as these systemic obstacles remain in place—including notions of parental responsibility, education, and gendered socialization according to gender-based stereotypes—, equal opportunity for women will continue to elude us.

9. Marie-Claude Lortie, "Légendes et bonnes ambitions," *La Presse*, September 9, 2016, www.plus.lapresse.ca/screens/4cb3bacl-eddb-4300-9cad-f994e4108480%7C_0.html, accessed September 19, 2016.

10. Many employers doubt the abilities of women, who then internalize this doubt. In an article titled "L'échec au féminin,"

published in November 2015 in *Châtelaine* magazine, journalist Marie-Hélène Proulx interviewed workplace psychologist and professor Hélène Lee Gosselin. The picture looks grim. "A few years ago, I compared career paths of eleven female vice-presidents to sixteen male vice-presidents working at the same three organizations . . . Men rose much quicker through the ranks. Their talent was noticed right away, they were quickly given important mandates, and the recognition by people in positions of power—often men—gave them the confidence to apply for promotions. But women usually rose within a company thanks to their own initiative. They put their heart into their work for a few years, then when they felt as though they'd exhausted all possibilities, they would look for a new position. . . . Women failed to receive the same level of social approval and reinforcement that makes us take risks and makes us feel worthy of aspiring to bigger things more quickly."

CHAPITRE 1. MOTHERHOOD AND THE JOB MARKET: THE DOMINION OF DISCRIMINATION

1. Amélie Daoust-Boisvert, "Une baisse de salaire due à sa maternité," *Le Devoir,* September 28, 2016, www.ledevoir.com/societe/sante/480976/medecin-enceinte, accessed September 28, 2016.

2. Pascale Navarro, *Femmes et pouvoir: les changements nécessaires. Plaidoyer pour la parité* (Montreal: Leméac Éditeur 2105; *Women and Power, The Case for Parity,* trans. David Homel (Montreal: Linda Leith Publishing, 2016), 96.

3. To restore a certain factual parity, the journalist could have put things into perspective by noting the systemic nature of the problem and wondering why it is always women who take parental leave, why as a society we believe this to be self-evident and take it for granted. Or mention the fact that taking parental leave may negatively impact a woman's career.

4. Fortunately, in the September 2016 issue of *Véro* magazine, Louis Morissette made a sort of public mea culpa in his column "Le dernier mot" by admitting that "gender inequality

still exists. It's just more underhanded, more insidious, even more hypocritical."

5. See Table 1.

6. Agence QMI, "Québec annonce une baisse des cotisations au RQAP," *Le Journal de Montréal*, September 9, 2015,www.journaldemontreal.com/2015/09/09/quebec-annonce-une-baisse-des-cotisations-au-rqap, accessed September 19, 2016.

7. Noémie Mercier, "Les vertus du congé de paternité," *L'actualité*, October 16, 2015, www.lactualite.com/societe/les-vertus-du-conge-de-paternite-2/, accessed September 19, 2016.

8. Ian Bussières, "Congés parentaux: le modèle québécois cité comme l'un des meilleurs du monde," *Le Soleil*, June 7, 2015, https://www.lesoleil.com/actualite/conges-parentaux-le-modele-quebecois-cite-comme-lun-des-meilleurs-du-monde-faoc4f267c8ab2ee1899ac29dec3606c, accessed September 19, 2016.

9. Valérie Harvey, "Les clés de la natalité," *La Presse*, September 19, 2014, www.plus.lapresse.ca/screens/dadbbb45-8f65-477f-92ec-b65d80362571%7C_0.html, accessed September 19, 2016.

10. Interview with Rachel Chagnon, professor in the Département des sciences juridiques at the Université du Québec à Montréal and director of the Institut de recherche et d'études féministes (IREF), conducted on June 8, 2016.

11. Ibid.

12. Term coined by Karl Marx to describe a working class unaware of the problems linked to social class. To use more modern language, this means financially unstable low-wage earners who are having trouble balancing a personal life with long hours of low-paid work.

13. Interview with Rachel Chagnon, op. cit.

14. Ibid.

15. The *Act Respecting Labour Standards* states that "distinctions in work conditions based on seniority, professional qualifications, experience, performance or evaluation quality are permitted." Punishing a female employee for taking a long parental leave by a poor evaluation that undervalues

her performance or experience is one tactic used by abusive employers.

CHAPITRE 2. WHY ARE MOTHERS STILL THE DEFAULT PARENT?

1. These benefits have changed names several times since they were initially introduced. In July 2016, the Trudeau government renamed them the "Canada child benefit."

2. This practice was abolished in Quebec scarcely a decade ago with the creation of the QPIP. Clearly, sexist attitudes of yore die hard!

3. Marilyse Hamelin, *La semaine rose,* 2017, www.lasemainerose.blogspot.ca/, accessed September 19, 2016.

4. Marilyse Hamelin, "L'inquiétude, le labeur des mères?" *Planète F,* September 17, 2015, www.planetef.com/dossier/parents-etes-vous-egaux/linquietude-le-labeur-des-meres/, accessed September 19, 2016.

5. Conseil du statut de la femme, "Pour un partage equitable du congé parental," April 2015, www.csf.gouv.qc.ca/wp-content/uploads/avis_partage_conge_parental.pdf, accessed September 19, 2016.

6. Side note: contrary to what is generally recognized and recorded by statisticians defining a single-parent family as one headed by a single father or mother with primary custody of one or more children, my unofficial and subjective definition of single-parenthood includes a parent raising a child alone for all or most of the time as well as a parent raising a child with joint custody. For example, a single mother who has custody of her child every other week is, within the scope of this definition, head of the family. On the weeks she spends with her child she must do everything on her own: meals, bath, bedtime, etc., which is no small task. The same goes for her ex-partner (if he is single, otherwise it would be considered a blended family).

7. According to the 2011 census, 75 percent of single-parent families in Quebec were headed by a woman (as per official criteria for primary custody and not my personal definition in the previous note).

8. Statistics Canada, "Understanding public-private sector differences in work absences," March 3, 2016, www.statcan.gc.ca/pub/75-006-x/2013001/article/11862-eng.htm, accessed September 19, 2016.

9. Ministère de la Famille et des Aînés, "Un portrait statistique des familles au Québec," 2011, www.mfa.gouv.qc.ca/fr/publication/documents/sf_portrait_stat_complet_11.pdf, accessed September 19, 2016.

10 10. Interview with Marianne Prairie, author, blogger, family and parenting speaker, and mother of two young children, conducted July 6, 2016.

11. Ibid.

12. Marie Pagès, "Le congé maternisant ou Comment le congé de maternité vous transforme en parfaite mère de famille," *Le Devoir,* July 14, 2016, www.media2.ledevoir.com/societe/actualites-en-societe/475412/le-conge-maternisant, accessed September 19, 2016.

13. Ibid.

14. Out of fifty bloggers total, *TPL Moms* contributors include forty-seven women and three men, accessed January 4, 2016.

15. Marc-André Durocher, "L'invulnérabilité n'est pas une qualité," *Planète F,* January 4, 2017, www.planetef.com/blogue/papa-marginal/, accessed January 4, 2017.

16. Interview with Olivier Lamalice, researcher for the Conseil du statut de la femme and author of the report "Pour un partage équitable du congé parental," conducted July 8, 2016.

17. Ibid.

18. Interview with Rachel Chagnon, op. cit.

19. Ibid.

20. Ibid.

21. A concept popularized in a sketch by comedian François Morency several years ago that refers to rewards programs such as Air Miles. The idea behind "Air Looses" is that a heterosexual man in a relationship accumulates rewards points when he makes his spouse happy, which allow him to go out or do things his "better half" doesn't necessarily approve of.

22. Karl Rettino-Parazelli, "La moitié du monde (du travail) est une femme," *Le Devoir*, March 4, 2016, www.ledevoir. com/economie/actualites-economiques/464603/8-mars-la-moitie-du-monde-du-travail-est-une-femme, accessed September 20, 2016.

23. Laval roundtable discussion on the feminine condition, "La conciliation travail-famille: c'est le temps, maintenant!" 2012, www.tablelaval.typepad.com/files/guide-concilia-tion-travail-famille-tclcf.pdf, accessed September 20, 2016.

24. Morgane Miel, "Trentenaires au bord du burn out," *Le Figaro*, January 30, 2016, www.madame.lefigaro.fr/societe/ trentenaires-au-bord-du-burn-out-280815-97922, accessed September 20, 2016.

25. Julie Miville-Dechêne, *Carte de visite*, TFO, 2014, www. tfo.org/fr/univers/carte-de-visite/100441874/julie-miville-dechene-presidente-du-conseil-du-statut-de-la-femme-du-quebec, accessed September 20, 2016.

26. "Le mythe de la femme parfaite: une création féminine," *Plus on est de fous, plus on lit!*, ICI Radio-Canada Première, October 9, 2013, www.radio-canada.ca/util/postier/sugger-er-go.asp?nID=1290573, accessed September 20, 2016.

27. Doc. Mailloux is a controversial psychiatrist, whose licence to practice was withdrawn by the Collège des médecins du Québec for racist remarks on a popular television program.

28. Author, actor, and playwright Steve Gagnon wrote a memorable essay on toxic masculinity, which I cannot recommend enough: Steve Gagnon, *Je serai un territoire fier et tu déposeras tes meubles*, (Montreal: Atelier 10, 2015), 77.

29. Out of curiosity I asked the Canadian Red Cross, which offers babysitting courses in schools and communities, whether there was a gender preference for the courses. Geneviève Déry, spokesperson for the organization's Quebec branch, confirmed that the course is more popular among girls. She explained, "since there is no certification or certificate issued, there are no official statistics, but the course continues to attract a large majority of girls—they are the ones who express interest." This is hardly surprising, since

their whole social circle reinforces the idea that caring for children is a female responsibility.

30. Interview with Olivier Lamalice, op. cit.

31. Annie Cloutier, *Aimer, materner, jubiler. L'impensé féministe au Québec,* (Montreal: VLB Éditeur, 2014), 232.

32 "The discovery of how germs affect the outbreak of infectious diseases at the end of the 19th century, thanks to the work of Louis Pasteur and other pioneers in microbiology, helped trigger a public health movement across Quebec." (Denis Goulet, "Le mouvement hygiéniste au Québec," *Cap-aux-Diamants: la revue d'histoire du Québec,* Vol 70, 2002, p. 17-20.) "To curb the high rate of infant mortality, the government is recommending a series of health initiatives, the most effective being milk stations . . . a program that aims to provide mothers with advice on nutrition and personal hygiene and give their children a ration of quality milk to prevent the spread of deadly bacteria." ("Ouverture des premières Gouttes de lait à Montréal," *Bilan du siècle,* Université de Sherbrooke, www.bilan.usherbrooke.ca/bilan/pages/evenements/187.html, accessed January 3, 2017.)

33. Geneviève Petterson, "La fin des vacances ou Comment je n'en peux plus de la morale sur Facebook," *Châtelaine,* July 25, 2016, www.fr.chatelaine.com/blogues/la-fin-des-vacances-ou-comment-je-nen-peux-plus-de-la-mere-parfaite/, accessed September 20, 2016.

34. In January 2013, a very divided Supreme Court (5-4 margin) upheld Quebec's civil code provisions for the Eric v. Lola case when it ruled that common-law spouses are not entitled to child support and other rights given to married couples. The ruling notes, however, that common-law spouses face discrimination in the event of a separation. Quebec is the only Canadian province that does provide for spousal support upon termination of the union. Yet Quebec has the highest rate of common-law spouses in the country. The current system is unfair to the lower of the two earners, often the woman, who in most cases ends up with either full or joint custody of the children. It is not uncommon to see a man work and save money for years—all while his

partner worked part-time or not at all in order to care for the children—, only to leave the family without providing any financial compensation to the woman, even though she made huge sacrifices. The current recommendation to protect against such situations is to draft a notarized agreement—a provision most couples don't make. This is why I believe we should give common-law spouses of two years the same rights and responsibilities as married couples, even if it means providing recourse for opting out in the case of a notarized contract. We have to turn the problem on its head to put things in their rightful place, once and for all.

35. Interview with Rachel Chagnon, op. cit.
36. Ibid.
37. Ibid.

CHAPITRE 3. INVOLVED DADS: OBSTACLES AND PREJUDICE

1. I had to request this information from the Conseil de gestion de l'assurance parentale since this data was not available in any of the published reports. We already know that 85 percent of Quebec fathers take paternity leave. Of these, more than a third don't take it when the child is born.

So when do they take it? There are two peak periods of the year. The first is in July and August, right in the middle of summer vacation. Fathers are respectively three times and two times more likely to take their paternity leave in July (construction holiday) and August than in April or October. The second uptick in paternity leave is in December and January, which coincides with the holiday season and the end of the year. Double the number of fathers take paternity leave in December and January as compared to April or October.

2. Conseil de gestion de l'assurance parentale, "Retombées économiques et sociales du Régime québécois d'assurance parentale," 2016, www.cgap.gouv.qc.ca/publications/pdf/RQAP_bilan_10ans.pdf, accessed February 2, 2016.

3. "Congédié pour un congé de paternité?" ICI Radio-Canada Québec, April 16, 2016, www.ici.radio-canada.ca/nouvelle/776361/paternite-congediement-houston, accessed January 6, 2017.

4. Things have since changed; parental leave of up to eighteen weeks for elected city officials was instituted in 2016.

5. Jean-Philippe Pleau, "Vivre sa paternité dans la dignité," *Le Devoir,* March 11, 2015, https://www.ledevoir.com/opinion/idees/434024/vivre-sa-paternite-dans-la-dignite, accessed September 19, 2016.

6. Interview with Jean-Philippe Pleau, director at ICI Radio-Canada and co-host of its show *C'est fou,* conducted June 9, 2016.

7. Sainte-Foy's Centre mere-enfant Soleil is affiliated with the Quebec City's Centre hospitalier de l'Université Laval. It offers services in pediatrics, neonatology, and prenatal counselling.

8. Interview with Jean-Philippe Pleau, op. cit.

9. Every year since 1996, the contest *Hat's Off to You!* showcases the courage and determination of women enrolled in a vocational training or technical training program leading to a career in a traditionally male-dominated occupation. Organized across Quebec by the Ministry of Education and Higher Education, it targets both high school and college students in public and private institutions.

10. Interview with Christine Fréchette, director of Public Affairs and External Relations at Montréal International and outspoken feminist, conducted June 7, 2016.

11. *Faut en parler: Casques roses,* Télé-Québec, 2016, written by Karina Goma and Karina Marceau, directed by Karina Goma, www.fautenparler.telequebec.tv/emissions/casques-roses, accessed September 20, 2016.

12. "Political parties, boards of directors, finance executives: all-male decision-makers are still widespread, and digital culture is undoubtedly a contributing factor. It is a sector in which women stand out for their absence. They make up only 10 percent of practicing engineers in Canada, and the vast majority work in chemical or biomedical engineering while computer and software engineers are still heavily male-dominated." (Marilyse Hamelin, "Arts numériques: place aux féministes!" *Gazette des femmes,* February 22, 2017, [www.gazettedesfemmes.ca/13669/arts-numeriques-place-aux-feministes/, accessed February 28, 2017].)

13. Interview with Laurent Turcot, Canada Research Chair and history professor at Université du Québec à Trois-Rivières, conducted May 31, 2016.

14. Ibid.

15. Ibid.

16. In July 2015, the rapper Koriass (aka Emmanuel Dubois) published a powerful piece in *Urbania*, "Natural Born Féministe" (www.urbania.ca/210104/je-connais-une-fille/), that recounted his wife's sexual assault in a denunciation of rape culture (including the trivialization of sexual assault, questionable humour, and victim blaming). Following its publication, he teamed up with former CSF president Julie Miville-Dechêne and myself in the spring of 2016 to speak at colleges about sexual consent as part of the presentation *Sexe, égalité et consentement.*

17. Interview with Jean-Philippe Pleau, op. cit.

18. Interview with Olivier Lamalice, op. cit.

19. Ibid.

20. Conseil du statut de la femme, "Pour un partage équitable du congé parental," op. cit.

21. Interview with Olivier Lamalice, op. cit.

22. Interview with Olivier Lamalice, op. cit.

23. Conseil du statut de la femme, "Pour un partage équitable du congé parental," op. cit.

24. Ibid.

25. www.theatlantic.com/magazine/archive/2012/07/why-women-still-cant-have-it-all/309020/, accessed September 20, 2016) highlighted how women have still not achieved equal opportunity and find themselves torn between career and family. It was met with huge success. Slaughter has since published the book *Unfinished Business* as a follow-up to her article.

26. Andrew Moravcsik, "Why I Put My Wife's Career First," *The Atlantic,* October 2015, www.theatlantic.com/magazine/archive/2015/10/why-i-put-my-wifes-career-first/403240/, accessed September 20, 2016.

CHAPITRE 4. SHARING PARENTAL LEAVE—
A RADICAL STEP?

1. The QPIP as we know it is the hard-won result of progressive Quebec forces. In *Retombées économiques et sociales du Régime québécois d'assurance parentale* (Social and economic impact of the Quebec Parental Insurance Plan), published by the Conseil de gestion de l'assurance parentale in December 2016, Marie-Ève Girous writes that, "beginning in the early 1990s, numerous groups advocating for women's and family rights called for an improved system of parental leave and a more accessible and generous parental insurance plan, one better suited to the reality and needs of Quebec families. In response, these groups formed the Regroupement pour un régime québécois d'assurance parentale. The collective, a CSN (Confederation of National Trade Unions) initiative founded in 1990, was made up of sixteen organizations, primarily family advocacy associations, women's rights groups, and trade union coalitions. It claimed to represent more than a million people across the province—both unionized and not, salaried and self-employed—concerned about the living conditions of women and Quebec families."

2. Interview with Christine Fréchette, director of Public Affairs and External Relations at Montréal International and outspoken feminist, conducted June 7, 2016.

3. Ibid.

4. Ibid.

5. Ibid.

6. Ibid.

7. Ibid.

8. Conseil de gestion de l'assurance parentale, "Retombées économiques et sociales du Régime québécois d'assurance parentale. Bilan de dix ans d'existence," (Social and economic impact of the Quebec Parental Insurance Plan, 10 years on), 2016, www.cgap.gouv.qc.ca/publications/pdf/RQAP_bilan_10ans.pdf, accessed February 2, 2016.

9. OCDE/OECD, Social Policy Division, Directorate of Employment, Labour and Social Affairs, Use of childbirth-related leave by mothers and fathers (2016).

10. Conseil du statut de la femme, "Pour un partage équit-able du congé parental," April 2015, www.csf.gouv.qc.ca/wp-content/uploads/avis_partage_conge_parental.pdf, accessed September 20, 2016.

11. Léger Marketing, "Sondage auprès des pères ayant eu recours au Régime québécois d'assurance parentale," August 2011, www.cgap.gouv.qc.ca/publications/pdf/Rapport_RQAP_peres.pdf, accessed March 7, 2016. Zins Beauchesne and Associates, "Sondage auprès de pères salariés ayant eu recours au Régime québécois d'assurance parentale (RQAP) à la suite d'une naissance. Rapport final," June 2014, www.cgap.gouv.qc.ca/publications/pdf/Sondage_peres_2014.pdf, accessed March 7, 2016.

12. Conseil du statut de la femme, "Pour un partage équitable du congé parental," op. cit.

13. Idem.

14. The policy whereby parents take leave in turn and not at the same time was meant to avoid the pitfall of the Quebec system: a father who takes leave while the mother is at home is never alone with the child in the role of primary parent.

15. Dominique Froment, "La France va inciter les pères à prendre un congé parental," *Les affaires,* August 6, 2014, www.lesaffaires.com/secteurs-d-activite/gouvernement/la-france-va-inciter-les-peres-a-prendre-un-conge-parental/571081, accessed September 21, 2016.

16. A parent can take up to fifty-two weeks of parental leave, but the QPIP only covers thirty-two; the extra weeks are unpaid. In rare cases, the weeks not covered by the QPIP are paid by the employer. See Table 1.

17. ICI Radio-Canada Première, *Pas de midi sans info,* May 8, 2015, www.ici.radio-canada.ca/emissions/pas_de_midi_sans_info/2014/archives.asp?date=2015/05/08&indTime=426&idmedia=7284732, accessed September 21, 2016.

18. It's no secret that equal pay remains an illusion. According to a 2011 Statistics Canada survey, revenue for women working full-time was just 75.3 percent that of their male counterparts.

19. Solange Collin, Denise Fortier, Carole Fréchette, Véronique O'Leary, Pierrette Savard, *Môman travaille pas, a trop d'ouvrage!* (Montreal: Éditions du Remue-Ménage, 1976), 78.

20. Interview with Olivier Lamalice, CSF researcher and author of the report "Pour un partage équitable du congé parental," conducted July 8, 2016.

21. See Table 1.

22. Interview with Olivier Lamalice, op. cit.

23. Interview with Christine Fréchette, op. cit.

24. Interview with Marianne Prairie, author, blogger, family and parenting speaker, and mother of two young children, conducted July 6, 2016.

25. Ibid.

26. Jean-François Chicoine and Nathalie Collard, *Le bébé et l'eau du bain. Comment la garderie change la vie de vos enfants* (Montreal: Québec Amérique, 2006), 513.

27. Interview with Marianne Prairie, op. cit.

28. Interview with Olivier Lamalice, op. cit.

29. Conseil de gestion de l'assurance parentale, "Retombées économiques et sociales du Régime québécois d'assurance parentale," op. cit.

30. Interview with Jean-Philippe Pleau, op. cit.

31. Ibid.

32. Interview with Laurent Turcot, op. cit.

33. Interview with Rachel Chagnon, op. cit.

34. Interview with Olivier Lamalice, op. cit.

35. In terms of flexibility, a self-employed woman entrepreneur such as a hairdresser or aesthetician could work part-time throughout her parental leave, even just one day a week so as not to lose her clientele, while still receiving QPIP benefits for the other days. These women would benefit from having access to reduced benefits spread out over time.

36. Interview with Olivier Lamalice, op. cit.

CHAPTER 5. ARE GENERATION Y/MILLENIAL PARENTS MORE EQUAL?

1. Interview with Rachel Chagnon, professor in the département des sciences juridiques at the Université du Québec à

Montréal and director of the Institut de recherche et d'études féministes (IREF), conducted on June 8, 2016.

2. Naël Shiab, "'Parce qu'on est en 2015,'" les femmes gagnent toujours moins que les hommes," *Métro*, November 29, 2015, www.journalmetro.com/actualites/national/873803/parce-quon-est-en-2015-les-femmes-gagnent-toujours-moins-que-les-hommes/, accessed September 21, 2016.

CONCLUSION. NECESSARY CHANGES

1. Eve-Lyne Couturier and Julia Posca, "Tâches domestiques: encore loin d'un partage équitable," Institut de recherche et d'informations socioéconomiques (IRIS), October 8, 2014, www.iris-recherche.qc.ca/publications/taches-domestiques, accessed September 21, 2016.

2. Entitled "Bébé, boulot, dodo... changer le monde!"

3. Let's not forget that Marie-Claire Kirkland was also the first woman in Quebec granted a national funeral . . . in 2016.

4. According to census data from 2011, 76 percent of single-parent families are headed by a woman.

5. I am aware that not every woman reads these books, and that some men do. But in most cases, it is still future mothers who do the research. And I know that these guides often contradict each other, but such literature sharpens parenting skills and therefore concerns fathers just as much as mothers.

6. Agence France-Presse, "Anne Hathaway nommée ambassadrice de bonne volonté de l'ONU," June 15, 2016, www.lapresse.ca/cinema/201606/15/01-4992234-anne-hathaway-nommee-ambassadrice-de-bonne-volonte-de-lonu.php, accessed May 4, 2017.

7. Naël Shiab, "L'assemblée nationale est sexiste et en voici la preuve," *L'actualité*, August 2, 2016, www.lactualite.com/politique/deputees/, accessed September 21, 2016.

8. See Table II attached.

9. Of course the father has a right to take these weeks in whole or in part, or to completely forgo them. The non-transferrable portion will be lost if not taken, as is the case with the current system's paternity leave.

Printed by Imprimerie Gauvin
Gatineau, Québec